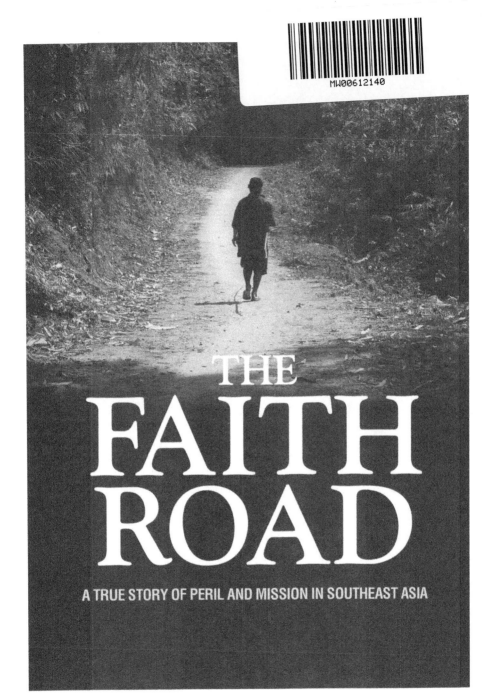

THE
FAITH
ROAD

A TRUE STORY OF PERIL AND MISSION IN SOUTHEAST ASIA

MEKONG
MULTIPLY

COLLEGE
P R E S S

The Faith Road is a truly amazing and fascinating account! If you have a missionary heart and a desire to pray for laborers to be sent to the fields that are white to harvest, you will be inspired and blessed! If you have always stayed in your comfort zone, this book will challenge and goad you to ask God where he wants you to share the love of Christ. I highly recommend this book.

— **Valerie Elliot Shepard**, daughter of Jim and Elisabeth Elliot and author of *Devotedly*.

Reading a book doesn't come naturally to me. If snails could read, they would lap me; they would leave me in their dust…or slime. But this isn't just *another* book. It is different. Perhaps it's because while reading of how God is moving right now in Laos, it has a uniquely similar feel to how God moved in the book of Acts. While *The Faith Road* is not divinely inspired, the stories have been inspired by the Divine.

They are true stories. Each account happened, and Eliot Branch was wise enough to give us a front row seat to see how God is using committed Christians and new believers to *reach the unreached.*

With each page I was reminded that God is *still* on the move and that the power of Jesus Christ can withstand and defeat any earthly stronghold, regardless of where you live and serve. If as an American Christian you aren't diligent, you become susceptible and can fall prey to a faith of convenience, to a comfortable Christianity. Jesus often asked his disciples, *"Where is your faith?"* And some two thousand years later I feel that through the pages of this book, I am being asked that same question.

I assure you that because of reading this book, my faith and boldness has deepened. So will yours, if you take the time to read it.

— **Dave Stone**, former Senior Pastor of Southeast Christian Church, Chairman of the Board of Spire Network.

It is not often that I read a book that is inspiring and insightful while also showing a depth of significant wisdom in the field of missions. *The Faith Road* shows all of these qualities and more. Eliot Branch has given us important insights from the field while also displaying a humble spirit that the Lord has blessed richly. You will be blessed as you see God at work in powerful ways among unreached peoples.

— **Dr. Christopher DeWelt**, Director of Intercultural
Studies at Ozark Christian College.

I don't care who you are, everyone loves a great missionary story; they're irresistible. I know of no other profession that experiences a greater encounter of clashes in culture than people who live in a distant place, adjust to a radically different worldview, and attempt to multiply followers of Jesus. Part of the appeal lies in how much we learn from the encounter of two cultures artfully organized in a well-told story. Here is an entire book full of that experience. The stories are vivid, powerful, well written and impactful. They are carefully ordered and crafted in such a way that we learn something from each one almost without realizing it is happening. That's what makes the group discussion guide at the end so crucial. The discussion questions are designed to provoke a conversation that will drive home the message of each chapter and lead us to grow in our faith and commitment to Jesus and his mission. I'm grateful to Eliot Branch for tracing out in brilliant, intriguing scenes what it means to follow the *Faith Road*.

— **Greg Pruett**, President of Pioneer Bible Translators.

Eliot Branch has done a remarkable job of drawing the reader into real-life, daily scenarios encountered by faithful followers of Christ. You will be inspired through his journey of faith as he seeks to make reproducing Christ-followers among all the tribes in Laos. You will be challenged by the paradigm shift emphasized by "Mr. Little" who exemplifies Jesus's model for making disciples. I look forward to heaven and being able to meet the faithful servants described in this book along with their generational disciples from Laos.

— **Tom Schneller**, Founder and Director of
Disciple Makers.

Eliot Branch likes to describe himself as very ordinary—but God has used him in absolutely extraordinary ways. His life inspires me, and this book really inspired me! It will have you on the edge of your seat as you read stories full of suspense and God's amazing faithfulness. You will be challenged to be persistent in prayer and bold in your witness, as you realize that "all tribes need to be engaged with the gospel" not only in Laos but wherever you live. A question that drove

Eliot was, "Do you want to be like Jesus?" If you do, read this book! You may even join the Red Thumb Society!

> — **Vince Antonucci**, Church Planter and Pastor of Verve Church, Author of *Guerrilla Lovers* and *God for the Rest of Us*, and Chaplain for the Las Vegas Golden Knights.

The Faith Road is more than the story of just one man. It is the story of the blood, sweat, and tears that become the seed of kingdom expansion. The adventures of faith challenge the status quo and raise the bar of mission.

Eliot is an advanced missiologist who understands and practices the latest innovations in communicating the timeless message of the gospel. Journey with him and our Lao national missionary partners as they face challenges in mission and witness the firstfruits of standing firm in faith.

> — **"Nick,"** Field Director of the Final 58.

The Bible tells us that God works in us as followers of Jesus both to will (desire) and to do (take action) his good pleasure. *The Faith Road* is a testimony to the faithfulness of God to carry out this work in his children. By sharing this story, Eliot Branch is modeling for us what it means to respond to God's faithfulness in full surrender and willingness to spend and be spent for Jesus. I am privileged to know some of the heroes of the faith in this modern-day recounting of the book of Acts in Laos. As you read, I am confident the Spirit of God will speak to your heart both to will and to do. Thank you, Eliot, for passing on to others what was passed on to you, that Laos and the world might know the Father has sent the Son.

> — **Lee Wood**, Preacher, Disciple, Missionary, Catalyst, and Founder of 1 Body.

The Faith Road is an exciting, enlightening and compelling book. It is memoir, devotion, chronicle, and commission, and a great joy to read. Jesus promised those who followed him "life deluxe" (John 10:10), by which he did not mean wealth and luxury but the life God created us for—loving and serving and sharing. When he said, "Follow me," those who heard traveled much, interacted with many diverse people, got thrown out of a few towns, and experienced the wonder of observing God at work and seeing people responding with joy to the message of the Kingdom. When Jesus left the earth, he told his disciples to "keep going" and they did. The book of Acts is a record of how Jesus's best friends likewise traveled much, interacted with many diverse people, got thrown out of a few towns, and experienced the wonder of observing God at work and seeing people responding with joy to the message of the Kingdom. In *The Faith Road*, Eliot Branch shares some very recent chapters in God's big story of contemporary disciples doing all these same things. Having known Mr. Branch for a few decades, I can attest that his passion is real and that these accounts are accurate. The Faith Road is sound Bible and sound missiology. I believe that the more Jesus-followers who spend time with this book, the sooner Christ's assignment to the Church will be fulfilled.

> — **Dave Embree**, Director of Christian Campus House at Missouri State University.

The Faith Road is a riveting account that provides a sobering reminder of how missionaries sacrifice their lives to bring the gospel to those who have never heard of Jesus. The testimonies of new believers and their journeys of faith will inspire the reader to take part in Jesus's Great Commission.

> — **Mey Siow Saephan**, Project Director of the Mien Bible Recording Project.

This won't be the first time, and I pray it's not the last, that someone identifies a movement of God as "Acts 29." No doubt it has applied to those situations; it certainly applies to this one. Reading this book is compelling, challenging, convicting. If you lack confidence that God is still moving, you won't any longer. If you wonder if God acts today, you'll be convinced. If you question whether or not God can use you, you'll emerge more compelled than ever to be a light where you are and to consider the possibility that God might move you somewhere else. If you come as one interested in God's work in the world, you will be blessed; should you lack interest, you won't by the time you finish.

> — **Dr. Chuck Sackett**, Preaching & Leadership Team at Madison Park Church, Professor of Preaching at Lincoln Christian University, Professor at TCMI, International.

L andlocked Laos, fabled "land of a million elephants," scene of exotic temples, opium runners, merciless bombing, communist incursion, rapid exodus of refugees—this is the backdrop for this epochal, fast-moving story. If you love Jesus and long to see his kingdom advanced to the last and least of the lost, then, like me, you will have trouble laying this book down.

Here you will read of young Lao and tribal Christians venturing forth, fearlessly facing hunger, thirst, arrest, brutal beatings to share Christ among peoples of many ethnic groups whose languages they did not know. These are modern day heroes of the faith like those you've read about in Hebrews 11:38 of whom "the world was not worthy."

These national missionaries have gone forth boldly two by two after the pattern Jesus, on two occasions, instructed His disciples to follow: "Take nothing for the journey—no staff, no bag, no bread, no money, no extra shirt" (Luke 9:3 NIV). "When you enter a house, first say, 'Peace to this house.' If someone who promotes peace is there, your peace will rest on them; if not, it will return to you. Stay there, eating and drinking whatever they give you..." (Luke 10:5-7 NIV).

In simple, down-to-earth biblical fashion after the manner of the apostle Paul, they have shared "the old, old story of Jesus and his love." They are seeing souls saved, new believers coming up from the waters of baptism with praises on their lips and joy in their hearts—and churches established.

Furthermore, these new believers are coming from forgotten people groups who have never before had the opportunity to hear the everlasting gospel even though twenty long centuries ago Jesus commanded us to "go and make disciples of all nations." Finally, here in this twenty-first century we can look forward with even greater expectation to seeing that "great multitude that no one could count, from every nation, tribe, people, and language, standing before the throne and before the Lamb" (Revelation 7:9 NIV).

Riveting, soul-stretching, challenging, inspiring—all fit this narrative well. My heart is ringing with praises for the miracles God is performing in Laos and for these who are giving their all for him.

> — **C.W. Callaway, Jr.,** Foreign missionary since
> 1948, and serving among the Iu-Mien in Southeast
> Asia and the Iu-Mien refugee community in the
> United States since 1950 to present.

The Faith Road is an up-close and personal account, which illustrates an example of current cutting-edge missions as well as describing one of the locations where the Lord is accomplishing amazing things in our day. It does not state broad principles but rather communicates through storytelling, which is far more engaging.

— **Curtis Sergeant**, Co-facilitator of 24:14.

Eliot Branch said yes to a dream that many would regard as impossible. A vision so big that he would need God himself to pull it off. As you read *The Faith Road*, you'll witness one of the boldest mission endeavors taking place in our world. The faithfulness and unwavering commitment of those involved will leave you inspired. But brace yourself, because God may want to use their stories to ignite a dream in you!

— **Caleb Bislow**, President of Unusual Soldiers,
Author of *Dangerous*

Fascinating! Eliot is an engaging storyteller able to capture the imagination and interest of young and old alike. His gripping accounts of God's activity in Laos are inspiring. Readers will be challenged to live by faith and to examine their own level of trust in God. The blend of what this ministry is doing in Laos and why they are doing it that way offers a transferable methodology and practice for the church everywhere.

— **Andrew "Fitz" Fitzgibbon**, Lead Minister at
Okolona Christian Church

I think it would be an honor to be arrested and imprisoned for the Lord." These are not words you and I speak, or even think about, often. Certainly, we do not hear them spoken in church, but they are words that scripture promises would and should be spoken. They are words brothers and sisters living today demonstrate with their faith, actions and the ultimate sacrifice. The man who spoke these words lived in Southeast Asia. He was later arrested, handcuffed and whisked away. His wife and son would never hear from him again—ever.

"God does not promise to keep us from rivers and fire. In fact, he will lead us into all of them. The more we follow in the footsteps of Jesus, the more rivers and fire we will face. His promise, however, is that he will bring us through." Such are the stories and principles punctuated by faith-filled exploits that Eliot Branch shares in his book, *The Faith Road*. Read it and then open the book of Acts—you will never be the same and your faith will never again be 'contained.'

> — **Mike Schrage**, President of Good News Productions, International

The *Faith Road* is a necessary reminder to the global church that '*panta ta ethne*' means '*panta ta ethne.*' Regardless of the population size or geographical location, every people group should have the opportunity to hear and respond to the gospel (2 Peter 3:9). The stories and events of what God has done and continues to do among the numerous tribes of Laos testify that although missiologists may label these people groups as unengaged and unreached, it does not mean they will resist the gospel. To the contrary, the stories and events of those who faithfully took the gospel to some of the remotest villages in Laos discovered that if followers of Jesus go and engage these unreached peoples, some seed will find good soil. The message for the global church is this: Many of these unengaged, unreached people groups are harvest fields. We have neglected to go. The Lao missionaries serve as a model that unreached does not mean they are unreachable. The journey may be long and tiresome and the task, at times, overwhelming. There will be opposition and persecution. Yet, we have the promise that Jesus will be with us to the end of the age.

> — **Dr. R. Bruce Carlton**, Professor of Cross-Cultural Ministry, Oklahoma Baptist University.

In *The Faith Road*, Eliot Branch captures the evidence of God's plan for missions, the personal call to "go," the physical hardships and challenges in logistics, and spiritual victories, while working in one of the most challenging fields in the world. Each step in the journey inspires the reader to rethink their own commitment of faith and calling, as well as how God is asking them to invest in their next mission field.

> — **Marina Bromley**, Author of *Morning Meditations at Marina's Kitchen Table: A Devotional Memoir.*

Bringing prayer and missions together has been a passion of mine for many years. *The Faith Road* goes beyond passion to practicality. The stories of God's intervention in Laos are a testament to the power of prayer and persistent faith.

> — **Dave Butts**, President of Harvest Prayer Ministries.

In the interest of full disclosure let me say missionary stories are a beloved genre. However, I always pick a fresh one up with trepidation. I've been disappointed—a reading experience akin to biting into a luscious peach only to find dry sawdust within. You long for it to be one of the great ones, but what a letdown when the book falls short.

Biting into *The Faith Road* produced all the bursting flavor and juice running down my chin that I could have hoped for. Eliot Branch narrates his story with an immediacy and authenticity that pulls the reader inexorably into a plot of heroically self-sacrificial attempts to penetrate places and peoples both mysterious and hostile to the gospel. As one who labored in the Asian Communist world, the cat and mouse with authorities rang especially true. The faith of stalwart workers and their disciples is inspiring—an example that is increasingly needed here in the West.

I was particularly thrilled with the approach of passing the apostolic task along to local Lao believers rather than curating it by the foreigners—the 222 Rule in practice: never do anything alone! Eliot faithfully follows Paul's command to Timothy in 2 Timothy 2:2: "And the things you have heard me say in the presence of many witnesses entrust to reliable people who will also be qualified to teach others" (NIV). These handoffs, which should be standard, happen infrequently enough to shine like stars in the missionary firmament when they are accomplished.

Thanks to these firsthand tales, I felt like I was present. The Lao church, described in these pages, will endure and impact many peoples and nations beyond tiny Laos. I cannot wait to meet them before the Lamb's Throne and relive these events with those who were there in the flesh.

> — **Brian Hogan**, Author of *There's a Sheep in my Bathtub*, President of Disciple Making Mentors.

THE
FAITH
ROAD

A TRUE STORY OF PERIL AND MISSION IN SOUTHEAST ASIA

ELIOT BRANCH

Your trial will be your chance
Luke 21:13

Mekong Multiply is a mission organization that exists to multiply disciples and churches among unreached people groups in Southeast Asia and beyond, by partnering with near-neighbor and national missionaries and equipping individuals and churches in effective missionary practices. For more information about the work and ministry of Mekong Multiply please contact us at missions@mekongmultiply.com or visit us online at www.mekongmultiply.com.

The Faith Road: A True Story of Peril and Mission in Laos
Copyright © 2021 by Mekong Multiply

Published by Mekong Multiply   &   College Press Publishing Co., Inc.
11700 Commonwealth Drive, Suite 100   2111 N Main, Ste C
Louisville, KY 40299   Joplin MO 64801

ISBN 978-0-89900-542-3

First printing 2021

To the greatest in the kingdom of heaven.

To those unknown faithful servants of Jesus who travel down the treacherous path, braving mountain and valley, nature and enemy, to proffer Christ's message of grace to those in darkness. To those who never receive praise, recognition, or honor on earth. To those about whom books are never written. To those whose witness has been forgotten.

Great is your joy in the world to come.

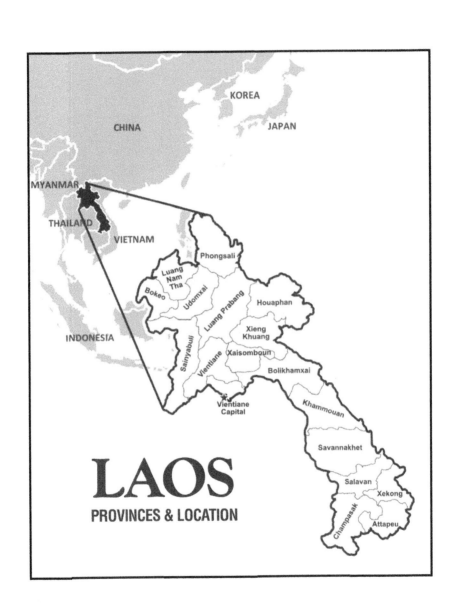

KOREA

CHINA

JAPAN

MYANMAR

THAILAND

VIETNAM

Phongsali

Luang
Nam
Tha

Bokeo

Udomxai

Luang Prabang

Houaphan

INDONESIA

Sainyabuli

Vientiane

Xieng
Khuang

Xaisomboun

Bolikhamxai

Vientiane
Capital

Khammouan

Savannakhet

Salavan

Xekong

Champasak

Attapeu

LAOS

PROVINCES & LOCATION

CONTENTS

FOREWORD

I beg you to hear my heart: this is not a book about missions for missionaries. This is a book for the church. This is a message for all Christians. This is a story for you.

To be certain, missions established the church. Missions exploded the Christian faith into the world through the obedience of early believers who took Jesus's command to heart. Without missions, across the street or across the ocean, the church dies. The church is both born *out of* missions and born *for* missions. For this reason, Eliot Branch's book, *The Faith Road,* belongs to the mainstream of Christian life and not simply pigeonholed to the arena of missions and missiological training.

I hope that all believers will read this book. My concern is the proclivity of the Christian community to relegate such a powerful work as *The Faith Road* to only missiological readership. It would be a disservice to the church for this book to end up being read solely by those who are already planning deep involvement in missions, are currently serving as missionaries, or are teaching such principles to others already interested in missions as a lifestyle. Inasmuch as missions is not reserved only for specialists, *The Faith Road* is a book for every follower of Christ.

The reality is this: in Matthew 28:18, the scripture that the church has dubbed the Great Commission, Jesus commands his followers to go from Jerusalem through Judea, through Samaria, and to all the people groups covering the earth. Unfortunately, the church in the West has often taken Jesus's command to go, which is non-negotiable, and changed it into a future, mystical "call." His command to go, however, is for all believers. The essence of a "call," therefore, determines *where*, not *if*, one shall go for a certain season of life.

The Faith Road represents the heart of God for every tongue and tribe on earth. When Jesus shared his succinct mission statement in Luke 19:10, he said that he "came to seek and to save the lost" (NIV). This very mission continues with our participation in the Great Commission.

To understand the spiritual battle we face, it is helpful to view the Great Commission from evil's perspective. After three and a half decades of overseas service in some of the most non-Christian environments on the planet, I believe my family and I have experienced the heart of evil. Our unique experience grants us this insight: Satan has his own mission with two primary goals. The first is to deny as many peoples of the earth as possible from gaining access to the loving grace found in Jesus Christ. Evil's second goal is to silence us. If families are fortunate enough to have access to the Good News and believe in Christ, evil's desire is to influence followers of Jesus to keep it to themselves. Often this is accomplished through covert and overt persecution. Evil aggressively works to make us keep the love that we have found in Jesus to ourselves.

Can we pause for a moment? If we, as Christians, keep our witness to ourselves, whose mission are we serving? Ouch!

Here is where Eliot's book is strong and masterful. He makes a clear case that the Great Commission is a command from Jesus that *must* be done. Secondly, he details vividly that the Great Commission—taking the Good News to every tongue and people group on earth—is a task that *can* be done.

The Faith Road is representative of what Jesus and his followers have accomplished throughout history. It also highlights the huge unfinished task before the church today. Almost half of the world's current population have little or no access to the love that is found in Jesus. After more than two thousand years of Christian history, the opportunity to give a cup of cold water in Jesus's name remains immense. Scores of books have been written explaining why this remains the case. At the heart of the matter, perhaps, is a lie from Satan that many in the church have believed regarding the Bible and missions. The lie sounds something like this: "The Bible is the Word of God. It is authoritative and powerful. It is a clear and perfect historical record of what God *used* to do." The implication is clear: evil readily allows for our believing in the trustworthiness and power of the Bible as long as it is read in *past tense*!

Conversely, Eliot Branch's book richly details the activities of God in the present active tense. *The Faith Road* reminds the reader that everything God has ever done in the Bible he continues to do in the present time! Simply put, to be on mission with God is to understand that the powerful God of history is the same powerful God who commands and empowers us to go today. His mission in the world is not yet completed, and he is not finished with us. God both enables us to discern his leading in our lives' current seasons and equips us to go now just as he equipped his earliest followers to go then. In the present time, and together with all the saints, God is calling us to change the course of human history.

Yet, there are many more rich takeaways from Eliot's book. He reminds us that the role of the pastor/teacher is one of a local shepherd who cares for the sheep who have been gathered into the kingdom of God in a specific location. In contrast, Eliot recaptures the central aim of the evangelist and church planter whose primary role, as detailed in Matthew 10:16, is to be a "sheep among wolves" rather than a "sheep among sheep." Disobedience to carrying out the Great Commission of Jesus Christ is to increasingly withdraw from the wolves and ignore those with little or no access to the Good News of Jesus.

Likewise, *The Faith Road* is a wonderful mix of biblical inspiration and exerted perspiration. It is obedience to a God-breathed command. It is also a commitment to put one foot, often blistered, in front of the other, traveling over mountains and through rivers. It is a testimony of how trusting God and his Word that our blessings upon those we have just met will, by faith, open both doors and hearts. Biblical verbal blessing bestowed upon those to whom God has led will provide the servant of God a meal to share, a place to sleep, and an opportunity for long spiritual conversations.

The Biblical narrative is mirrored in this contemporary account of amazing adventures in the mountains and valleys of Laos. Faith journeys begin on treacherous roads to remote villages and blossom through shared meals between believers and those waiting to believe. Faith is born and housed, as it was in the New Testament, in homes. The unreached peoples of the earth have not believed simply because they have not heard. Additionally, *The Faith Road* constantly reminds us that the cost of following Jesus is steep. Persecution has always been faith's travel companion.

The Faith Road serves us, the church, well. It is a clear road map, whether we are trusting Jesus by walking across the street where we currently reside or by crossing the oceans for the sake of those with little or no access to his Good

News. It is a testimony that echoes the Biblical narrative, allowing the reader to embrace the very essence of God's heart—that those who have never heard would be given the chance to believe.

— **Dr. Nik Ripken**
President, Nik Ripken Ministries
2021

NOTE TO THE READER

The stories you are about to read are all true. None of the events or people are fictional. All of the miracles of God and actions of the described parties are actual and not embellished. Many details of the circumstances are omitted for brevity or summarized for narrative flow.

Except for historical and public figures, every name in this book is a pseudonym, including the author's. Real names of individuals, both expatriate and Lao, are never used. Village names are also pseudonyms. Provinces and cities are actual, but none of the many mission agencies, organizations, churches, financial partners, or local companies are named in this book. Omission of the names of all partners and organizations is intentional.

The author and publisher feel it was important to obscure the identity of all partners for two reasons. First, for security. Many of the individuals described in this volume are still active mission participants in the field. As such, they face daily the risk of persecution, arrest, or expulsion. Second, for credit. We are grateful to all parties who have contributed to the work yet feel it best to allow God alone to receive praise for what he has done in Laos. Omitting names of both individuals and organizations from this published work helps us to accomplish this goal in a consistent manner.

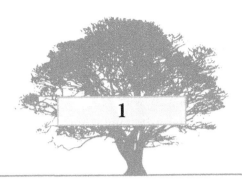

THE RED THUMB SOCIETY

My heart was beating heavily. It was five in the morning and I couldn't sleep. Thoughts kept racing through my head. *Is it the jet lag?*

I had returned from America to the small Southeast Asian country of Laos just two days before. I had immediately driven north, through the mountains, to the province of Xieng Khuang, near the Vietnamese border. Five in the morning here is five in the evening back home. My body's clock was out of whack. Yet there was more to my insomnia than just the jet lag.

I couldn't get my thoughts past it. This is what happens when you delay the inevitable, when you anticipate a confrontation. You can't stop thinking about it. I just wanted it to be over, but there was nothing I could do. I couldn't make the clock tick any faster. *What's going to happen? What should I do?*

Go for a run.

To where? It was still dark outside. There are too many potholes on the streets in Laos and too much debris to navigate safely. The roads are narrow and the traffic is crazy…. *Well*, I realized, *it's not so crazy at five in the morning*. This was actually a good time to run—few cars and cool air. I just needed to watch my steps. The anxiety motivated me. *Okay, I'll do it. I will run the six miles out to the Plain of Jars and back. I need to burn off this nervous energy!*

As I laced on my running shoes, I contemplated all the events from the day before. My mind could not focus on anything besides the incident that had shaken me and kept me from sleeping in peace.

A friend of mine, Pastor Woun, was a leader in the Hmong church here in Xieng Khuang. He had invited me to conduct a special training to a group of Hmong believers. I was casting a vision for what it would take to reach all the tribes in Laos. And I was eager to recruit Hmong brothers and sisters for this task. We had communicated via private messages during the previous month, and all the details had been arranged. Now the time had come.

This particular Hmong church ran a government-authorized Bible Training Institute on the upper level of their building. The pastors showed me the official government certificates, stamped with red seals, which they had proudly displayed on the wall of the primary training room. Their boldness impressed me. They did not appear to have any qualms about worshiping Christ openly.

The Hmong are a special tribe in Laos. Occupying the elevated plateau of Xieng Kuang province with its anomalous grasslands and pine tree forests, the Hmong possess a temperament distinct from the Lowland Lao majority. They are hard workers, passionate and decidedly industrious. Moreover, the Hmong have a history of opposing the communist regime.

During the Secret War in Laos, which ran concurrently with the Vietnam War, the United States of America funded a covert military campaign operated by the Central Intelligence Agency instead of the US Armed Forces. Its purpose was to oppose the communist troops of North Vietnam from encroaching into the territories of Laos. The Hmong were the principal players equipped and supported by the CIA. In spite of international agreements to keep Laos neutral, both the Soviet-backed Viet Cong and the American-backed Hmong fought bloody battles on these same plains where I now stood. Few Americans are familiar with this history, and even fewer realize how the effort decimated the impoverished nation of Laos.

What the Hmong lacked in conventional military training and sheer numbers against the superior Viet Cong forces, they made up for in bravery, courage, and knowledge of the local terrain they were defending. They also had one more thing the Viet Cong did not—American bombers at their beck and call.

And call they did. Flying out of bases in Thailand, American bombers went on nonstop carpet-bombing runs that reduced villages of grass and bamboo houses to smoldering heaps of sticks and ashes. The campaign lasted from 1964 to 1973, and more than 270 million bombs obliterated the mountains and forests of Laos. The US carried out over 580,000 bombing missions during these nine years, which averaged to one every eight minutes. More bombs were dropped on this tiny, sparsely populated country than all the bombs that were dropped on Europe during World War II. Because a good portion of these bombs never detonated, the "bombies" (unexploded metal balls that look like toys) continue to maim and kill children who find them in the fields to this day.

In spite of the excessive bombing, the Americans and Hmong ultimately failed. The communists seized power over Laos, and a revolution was born. To the present time, Lao primary school teachers proudly indoctrinate their young students that Laos gained its freedom and independence in 1975 by defeating the American Imperialists. This was the Communist Revolution.

In the years following the war, tens of thousands of refugees fled the country, including more than fifty thousand Hmong. They migrated to Thailand and eventually the US. Those left behind, on the other hand, became a persecuted minority group. The new Lao government was especially suspicious of Hmong Christians, who were numerous, thanks to a movement of Hmong people who turned to Christ in the 1950s. In the view of the communist authorities, Hmong Christians had accepted the religion of the enemy.

So here I was, an American man standing in front of a large group of Hmong Christian leaders in the heart of the province that was once the primary battlefield in a proxy war between the world's two superpowers of the day. If the Lao communists were going to be suspicious, we had all the red flags. Though our purpose was not political, religion can easily be construed as such and often is.

Pastor Woun asked me to arrive early the first day. The village headman of their city neighborhood (called villages in Laos) wanted to use the large church building for a community meeting that morning. It would be impolite to refuse, and the church's large building provided the ideal meeting place for the village. Consequently, Pastor Woun wanted me to arrive at least two hours before they began, so I could discreetly climb to the upper level and remain out of sight while the headman conducted business below. No need for the presence of a white *falang* to prompt questions from the village authorities. Pastor Woun assured me that all would be safe, and I complied, as I was accustomed to the need for secrecy.

I arrived at 6:30 a.m. and ascended the stairs to the church's upper level. Over the next two hours, the participants trickled in. I met some old friends and many new students enrolled there to study the Bible. When it was time to begin, more than thirty Hmong leaders from churches in three different provinces assembled to participate in my training. The turnout was unprecedented. They were mostly male but with a handful of young women. They sat upright in their chairs with smiles fixed upon their faces. A slight bow of the head accompanied each word of greeting they spoke as they introduced themselves. All the participants appeared eager and passionate about the Lord.

I began by casting a vision about how God views the world. I made the point that we should view the world in the same way. As Christians, our goal is to become just like Jesus. If we are like Jesus, we will care about the things Jesus cares about more than anything else. To understand what Jesus cares about, we looked at the Lord's Prayer. The first three requests in this prayer are requests for God's benefit, not our own. Jesus taught us to pray for what *he wants* before we pray for what *we want* and need. He wants his name to be honored as holy (hallowed), his kingdom to come, and his will to be done on earth as in heaven.

This discussion led to the fact that we should be concerned for all the lost people, villages, and tribes in Laos—people who have never heard the gospel—because Jesus is concerned about them. I wrote down the words Country, Province, District, Area, Village, Household, Person on the white board. I asked them to which level do we want to see a church planted. Everyone agreed that a church should be planted in every village. We estimated that there are approximately ten thousand unreached villages in Laos.

As I directed the participants to break into small groups and discuss how we might accomplish this goal, two men poked their heads through the doorway. They were policemen and wanted to talk with me. However, I did not recognize them as police officers, since the main one wore plain clothes. I only noticed the other man's uniform under his yellow coat after I walked outside. I wondered why no one else had recognized them as police and signaled me to stop before they entered the training room. Nonetheless, they were there now and asking me where I was from.

"I am American," I replied, and they asked to see my passport. I walked back into the room, through the students, who were mingling during the break. They still did not realize I was talking with the police. I fetched my passport and gave it to the lead officer. He was polite and said, "Okay, you can continue your lesson, and when you are finished, come into the police station to talk."

I returned to the room somewhat distraught. I mentioned to some of the students that the men who spoke with me were police officers and now I could go to jail. I asked if anyone had recognized them as police, but no one had. Then word that the police had come and confiscated my passport found its way to the pastors. They quickly climbed the stairs and called me into the back room.

Pastor Khan was quite concerned. He sat without speaking, thinking about what to do. Pastors Daopet and Woun entered the room as we got our bearings on what just happened. Pastor Khan suggested we discuss the issue with Pastor Sampan, who is not Hmong but Phuan, and serves at a different church in town. Pastor Sampan is the official head of the Lao church in Xieng Khuang province. So we headed to his office to ask for his advice.

On the way, Pastor Khan explained to me some recent history. There was jealousy in the Hmong church stemming from one man, a former teacher at the Institute. About a month before our training, he had a disagreement with the other pastors and angrily ripped his own picture from the wall, effectively resigning. Since that time, he had caused problems for the church.

Earlier in the morning, the wife of the disgruntled pastor drove by the church and noticed the women preparing for a large noontime meal. She queried one of the kitchen girls about the occasion, who replied that they were making lunch for Eliot, who had come to teach. The women invited her to help, but she said she was busy. Sometime later, others saw her husband dressed up and headed toward the police station. They wondered what business he might have there. Shortly after this, the police arrived and confiscated my passport.

It started to make sense. We knew it was unlikely that the police would notice our training on their own or have any interest. However, as is often the case, the police investigate and arrest Christians after someone nearby complains or reports them. Jealousy, in one way or another, is usually at the root of these situations.

Pastor Sampan did not offer much advice other than to admit the truth, apologize, and listen to what they had to say. After thanking Pastor Sampan for his input, Pastor Khan and I proceeded to the police station. When we arrived, a banquet had just begun, and all the staff were busy with the festivities. The officer who had taken my passport came out to meet us and said that it was not a convenient time. His boss, the Police Chief, was just beginning to eat and drink. He directed us to return at 8:30 the next morning.

Pastor Khan and I returned to the church in time for lunch. As we ate, we discussed the situation and what best to do. I posted a prayer request to my private Facebook "Prayer Force" group. Then I called my wife, Mali, who was at our home in the US. It was not a short conversation. She was upset and worried. Honestly, her words caused me more stress than the situation with the police. I did not know what to say to put her at ease. I asked her to trust God along with the rest of us. I prayed for her and asked others to pray for her too.

When I finished talking on the phone, the students found me and urged me to come teach. They reasoned, "Eliot, since you don't have to go into the police station until tomorrow, we can study now. Instead of being careful and hiding you upstairs, now we can be open since the police already have your passport!" So, I returned to teach and shared about how to prayer-walk and bless people, share the gospel, lead people to faith, and train new disciples to repeat the entire process. When we finished that evening, all the students and pastors prayed for me. They prayed for God to give me strength for the impending interrogation the following day. I retired to my guesthouse to clean up my phone's data and discard any compromising materials. I locked some files on my computer and phone and prepared to leave them with a friend during the next day's interrogation.

I woke up at 3:30 the next morning. The early rise was partly from jet lag and partly from anxiety in anticipation of facing the police. I checked messages and prayed. By the time I began my jog to the Plain of Jars, it was almost 5:30.

After the first mile, I could see the sky brightening with each footfall. The darkness turned to twilight, and by the time I approached my turn-around point, the sun had risen behind the clouds. In the light of the morning, I noticed a small troop of dogs at the end of the road. The dogs took note of me and all at once started to bark. They were agitated and intimidating as a pack. I had approached their turf, and they were mustering their voices in defense.

Dogs are brave when they are on their own turf. A dog that is off his turf is a scared dog—his tail is between his legs, and he is anxiously looking for a path back to safety. These dogs, however, were clearly emboldened to protect their own turf. Their barks were rather frightening, but I recalled some boyhood wisdom: dogs that bark are usually not the dogs that bite. I purposed to stand my ground and conceal any fear. Sure enough, as I ran toward them in confidence, they melted away. The dogs, as intimidating as they were, were actually scared of *me*.

The Lord gave me an epiphany: Dogs are not like tigers. Dogs protect their turf, but tigers take their turf with them wherever they go.

As I meditated on this analogy, God showed me that Satan is like a dog. He protects his turf. He is brave when he is on his own turf. He will bark and he will intimidate; he will threaten and accuse. He will work through menacing communist policemen to dispirit God's children. This is because people typically scramble in fear, as soon as Satan chirps, "Boo!" But often our fearful flights are unnecessary.

I realized that as the Lord's children, we are tigers. The Lord is with us wherever we go. Therefore, we have no reason to scamper, despite intimidation. I was heartened to have confidence in the Lord for my imminent interrogation with the police. They are messing with God's child here—*they* should be afraid!

I finished my run with more courage than I had begun. After showering, I deposited my computer and phone at the house of a friend, and drove to the church to meet Pastor Khan.

Pastors Khan and Daopet were waiting for me along with a few other Hmong leaders. They invited me into the back room of the church to pray before we headed to the police station. After I sat down, Pastor Khan articulated the following to me.

"Phonsavanh [the provincial capital of Xieng Khuang, where we were located] is like the city of Sodom in the Bible."

Okay, that was a bit unusual. I was not sure where he was going with this, but he continued.

"Two angels visited Lot there in the city of Sodom. Lot received his guests and took them into his house. Then the people of the city came to his door and demanded they turn the two men over to them because they intended to do wicked things. But Lot refused. He loved and protected his guests—so much that he even offered his two young daughters to placate the angry mob. These two men came under the protection of Lot's roof since they were his guests.

"Eliot, you are our guest here. We invited you, and we will protect you. Don't worry about anything. We will do the talking. We will go to the police station with you, and whatever they want to do to you, they will have to do to us. You are our guest, and we will stand with you through it all."

My eyes welled with tears. I choked up the entire time we prayed. I had been somewhat nervous and anxious about going into the police station but not really fearful. I trusted that somehow God would get us through it all. But Pastor Khan's words touched me deep in my heart. After posting my prayer request on Facebook the day before, many people left comments saying they were praying for me. Some just wrote the word "Praying!" or posted a prayer-hands emoji. I appreciated these expressions of concern and prayers for me.

However, Pastor Khan was going to go in there *with* me, stand with me, and was fully prepared to take the brunt of any blows I might receive. He was going to make my problem his problem. He was going to suffer with me. He would stand with me and stick with me no matter what.

Wow. I had never had anyone show me such love. So I cried.

After we finished praying, Pastor Khan hugged me and reassured me once more. Then we got into the car and drove over to the police station. After arriving, we met the same police officer who confiscated my passport the day before. He led us upstairs where we talked for a brief minute. Then, it was time for the interrogation.

As expected, they separated us and escorted me to the interrogation room. It was a tiny, separate, one-room building on the back corner of the lot. Five officers accompanied me into the small room then shut the door behind us. There were no windows on the front or sides of the room, so no one outside could watch or listen. There was one window on the back wall, which they left open. Through it, I could spy the lily pads on a small pond down below. Nothing hung on the walls except a large white paper traced out as a height scale for taking mug-shot photos of those arrested. There was one wooden desk in the room, a couple chairs behind it, and a bench in front of it. Two of them sat behind the desk, the younger one with the notebook and report forms and the other officer—the one who had first taken my passport—as the interrogator. I sat down on the bench. The other three officers stood beside and behind me.

This was not my first rodeo, as they say. I had experienced some similar events a couple times before and had stood with some of our Lao partners in the past as they endured such interrogations. I understood that the arrangement of the room, the position of the officers, and the entire interrogation approach was designed to intimidate. Intimidation is a technique to obtain confessions or find cracks in the stories of those accused. Even so, a pang of fear ran through my body knowing what some of my Lao brothers and sisters have faced in such interrogation rooms.

Then the words of King David came to mind: "The Lord is my light and my salvation—whom shall I fear? The Lord is the stronghold of my life—of whom shall I be afraid?" (Psalm 27:1 NIV).

I had planned to teach these words to the students the following day. The Spirit provided me a measure of courage as I remembered them.

The interrogator was serious but not mean. As he asked questions, the younger man recorded the information onto the forms. They spent half of the time going through my history. They began by saying, "Tell us everything you have done since you were eight years old." I found this somewhat humorous. What they meant, however, was from what years and ages I went to school, worked, and where I lived at each stage. They recorded the names, ages, and occupations of my parents, along with the same for my wife, children and siblings. They also asked about when I first came to Laos, what I did there, and for how long.

Of particular importance to them was what I was doing in the US before embarking upon my current trip to Laos. They suspected I worked for a church or Christian organization. I was able to tell them that I had a coffee roasting business and that I sold Lao and Chinese coffee, which anyone can see on our website. They noticed from my passport that I had been in China and noted that my roastery also sells Chinese coffee. It made sense to them.

Finally, we got into the issue at hand. They wanted to know how I came to Xieng Khuang and who invited me to teach. I gave the simplest explanation that connected all the dots in a truthful narrative without offering up the names of other expatriates or nationals not pertinent to the account. I explained that because I had been to Xieng Khuang many times in the past, had sourced coffee from there, and had collaborated with the Department of Agriculture, I knew many people. Additionally, I knew one of the teachers at the Bible Institute, a registered and authorized school, who used to be employed by a friend in another province: Pastor Woun. In Laos, when respected guests visit, Lao people will invite them to share their ideas and stories. It is a common cultural practice. Pastor Woun asked me to share mine. I obliged and was only there for a couple hours when the police arrived.

The interrogator recorded the entire narrative step by step. He repeated every question three or four times with a more serious look on his face, as if any statement I made was difficult to believe. I recognized this interrogation technique. They intended to see if I would alter my story in a way to make it more believable to the officers. However, I repeated my answers with the same information each time, only struggling with simple things that I just did not remember. (*Who stood up in front of the room first that morning?*) I had given them Pastor Woun's name, as he was my simplest connection to the Bible Institute. Without providing some connection, it would leave a significant hole in my account. I had indeed exchanged text messages with him in advance of my visit.

They asked me what I taught. I was prepared to preach an entire sermon to them. I began by explaining how Jesus lived and taught when he was on earth and how he prayed, "Not my will, but yours be done." I explained that he gave us an example of how to submit to God, the ultimate authority. Therefore, as his followers, we need to be like him. He taught us not to be selfish but to put others before ourselves—this includes other families, other tribes, and people from other countries.

I didn't get too far into my message when they cut me off. They had heard enough. All they wrote down in the report about the content of my teaching was, "He taught biblical principles."

The entire interrogation took around three hours. When we were finished, I was very thirsty. I hadn't had anything to drink since my morning jog. They did not offer me anything either. However, the entire time I did my best to maintain my composure. I was polite yet assertive in my answers.

When we were finished, they read the report back to me, line by line. As they read, they had me nod in agreement with everything they reported I had said. It was a brief summary but all in alignment with my testimony, so I signed at the bottom. Then they had me press my thumb onto a pad of red ink and mark my fingerprint in the margin next to each portion of the report.

My thumb was now stained red. I had thus joined "The Red Thumb Society" of Christians in Laos who had been arrested, detained, and booked for their witness about Jesus.

While I was being interrogated, Pastors Khan and Daopet were waiting in the main office. The police chief came through and Pastor Daopet recognized him as one of his nephews—a fellow Hmong person but not a believer. The chief commented to Pastor Daopet that the interrogation was taking a long time, wishing it were complete so that we could meet with him and wrap it up. Nevertheless, he needed to travel to another district and left. Before departing, however, he informed Pastor Daopet that the fine schedule for a religious offense is $500 to $1,000.

After my interrogation, they ushered me back to the main office where the pastors were waiting and allowed me to drink a cup of coffee. We spoke casually at this point as one of the police officers quizzed me about coffee cultivation. Since I had mentioned Pastor Woun in my testimony, they wanted to interrogate him too. So, Pastor Khan scurried off on a motorcycle to fetch Pastor Woun. We waited for Pastor Khan to return with Pastor Woun in the office with the other police officers. Never once did they smile at us. (As the "Land of a Million Smiles," which Laos is sometimes called, Lao police officers must undergo training on how to keep a straight face, since smiling is such an ingrained part of their culture.)

I knew and trusted Pastor Woun, but I didn't know how much experience he had with police interrogations. I hoped he wouldn't offer any information more than absolutely necessary or any other names and would intuitively arrive at the same simple narrative as I had shared. My testimony was completely truthful, though not exhaustive in information. I knew they would not allow me an opportunity to talk with Pastor Woun to "get our story straight" before he entered the interrogation room.

A few minutes later, Pastor Woun arrived and entered the office. The officer announced that they would interrogate Pastors Khan and Woun, and that Pastor Daopet and I could leave. The police chief had already departed and would not return until 2:00 or 2:30 that afternoon. They kept Pastor Khan in the main office to conduct his interrogation and led Pastor Woun outside toward the same interrogation room where I had been.

Meanwhile, Pastor Daopet and I were departing from the large two-story building. At the bottom of the stairs, the officer escorting Pastor Woun was called to do something and left Pastor Woun there to wait momentarily. This afforded me about 90 seconds to talk with him privately. I quickly reviewed with Pastor Woun the basic outline of my testimony, how I knew him, and how I was invited to share with the Bible students.

When Pastor Daopet and I arrived back at the church, we went into the back room to debrief and pray for a few minutes before lunch. All the students waited for us, praying on our behalf while we were gone, and were excited to see me walk back into the training room. Their concern and expression of love was touching.

During lunch, I asked Pastor Daopet if I could take a moment to share a few words with the group as they ate. He was happy to allow me the opportunity. I wanted to encourage them with words I had planned to teach the next day but now knew I would probably not get the opportunity to share.

"Brothers and sisters," I began, "do not be discouraged by this opposition! We know we must face these kinds of things because Jesus told us we would.

If we are not a threat to Satan, he won't bother us. But if our vision of a movement of disciples and churches multiplying to all the tribes and villages in Laos begins to come true, then we will most certainly face opposition and persecution! It is a given, and it is expected! In John's vision in Revelation 6, when the fifth seal was opened, he saw the souls of those who had been killed because of their testimony about Jesus. They cried out to God asking how long before he judges the world and avenges their blood. God gave them white robes and told them to wait a little while longer until the full number of those to be killed for maintaining their testimony about Jesus was complete. This means that more people will have to die before Jesus comes back! Jesus doesn't want anyone to perish but all to come to repentance. As we bring his message to the ends of the earth, many of us will be persecuted and some of us will even be killed. That is okay—Jesus told us it must be this way. We can be fearful, but we must not give in or give up! Our faith must overcome our fear. So please don't give up."

When I finished, Pastor Daopet and all the students jumped up and shouted, "Amen!" and raised their arms in the air. We finished our meal and then they implored me, "Eliot, we have about one and a half more hours before you need to return to the police station to see the police chief. Can you teach us during this time?" I agreed and proceeded upstairs to continue my lesson.

At 2:00 p.m., we all prayed and went back to the police station. The police chief still had not returned, so we sat and waited. We waited for more than an hour when the main interrogator walked out of the room and indicated the chief had finally returned. Then we continued our wait as the interrogator was presumably summarizing all the testimony to his boss before meeting with us.

Finally, around 4:30 p.m., the interrogator returned and announced that the chief would not meet us. Apparently, he was embarrassed, as he did not see anything in all three of our testimonies that was a great offense. It all matched. They indicated that we should have obtained a permission slip in advance, but they did not feel the violation was serious enough to proceed with official charges. After a few more formalities, they handed my passport to me and we were done. Then, for the first time, the interrogator smiled at us.

When we returned to the church, the pastors were elated! They felt it was a tremendous victory provided by the Lord. The pastors characterized our trials as a blessing—almost as if they were glad it happened. To my surprise, they had never faced opposition like this before. "The Lord has taught us how he will take care of us through trials, and now we are stronger as a result!" they rejoiced.

Enduring opposition has been the modus operandi for the church throughout the ages. A short history of Christian preference and prominence in the US is more of an anomaly than a historical status quo. But it has lulled some Christians into expecting an easy road. The Bible promises that if we wish to live a godly life we will be persecuted (2 Timothy 3:12). There is no way around it. The only way to live a comfortable Christian life, safe from persecution, is never to be a threat to Satan.

My vision to see all the tribes in Laos engaged with the good news of Jesus was most definitely a threat to the Enemy's stronghold.

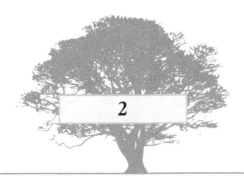

JESUS SAW ME

I am no one special.

Let me clarify. I believe that God has made us all special. I believe that his body is made up of many members, and every last part has a special role to play. I believe that we are all unique in the way we've been designed and, to the extent we submit to God's will and leading, we all are colorful pieces in the grand mosaic of diverse hues God is arranging together into his beautiful masterpiece. I truly believe this. And I don't know anyone wise enough to hold up a measuring stick to your mosaic piece and tell you how well you are hitting the mark. Who are we to judge another man's servant? I know I have too many planks to go around being a speck remover.

Judging other people is human nature. To be sure, it is a part of our *sinful* nature. We do it even when we are telling others not to do it. Those who complain that Christians are judgmental are probably passing judgment on Christians. Yet Christians are often guilty as charged, in spite of aspiring to the teachings of Jesus not to judge others. We, too, often fail. However, judging others is not solely a Christian tendency—it is a human one.

Most of us judge because we would like to feel that we are somehow, at least in some small way, superior to those around us. Fear that we may be inferior drives many of us ahead. Underlying this fear is the sense that if we are inferior—if we cannot offer anything to anyone that they could not get elsewhere—then we are unnecessary. If we are unnecessary, then why are we here? What purpose do we serve?

I was a sophomore in high school when these thoughts and questions hit me hard. I struggled to see my value in a dog-eat-dog society that praised people who had wealth, beauty, charisma, and talent. I did not possess these qualities in any remarkable way. I did not stand out.

I was not born into wealth. It never bothered me in a great way that my family could not afford things I saw other families could. It really did not, though I suspect my parents always wished they could have done more. They did a lot actually.

I am forever proud of my roots and being the son of a carpenter. I know my father always worked hard and with integrity. He always treated people right, did quality work, and was generous. He was a great example to me. Countless times, I have bragged about how my dad built the house in which I grew up. I had the honor of helping him build a house the summer after I graduated from high school as well as the family cabin at Rocky Top—a 10-acre plot of woods for camping, hunting, and fishing near Stockton Lake in rural southwest Missouri.

I am proud of my parents' example to take in my grandfather to live with us the last few years of his life. My dad built a nice apartment for his father out of our garage. I well remember Grandpa helping to dry the dishes as I washed them after the evening's meal. Each night he would strike a match under the edge of the counter, light up his pipe, and tell me stories of the "olden days" while we worked. I would cough a little each time he drew his first puff, which made him chuckle. I will never forget him telling me that my dad was a good man.

But life as a carpenter was tough when the winters arrived and work dried up. The utility company shut off our electricity once for falling behind on the bills. My father was understandably embarrassed and stressed. I, on the other hand, thought it was an adventure to eat off the old wood stove in the family room. It felt like camping. But it didn't last long.

Even so, I was never the kid who brought the latest toy from TV to show off at school or impressed kids with our gadgets when they visited. No one came to our house to swim in our pool or jump on our trampoline because, of course, we never had those things. Consequently, though I never doubted my parents' love for me in these matters, nothing about our family's wealth attracted attention or interest from others.

Neither did my appearance attract any attention. I was about as plain as could be. A time came in my early teens that I thought if I could just comb my hair the right way or dye it blonde, then perhaps I could draw more interest. I never dyed it, but it didn't take me too long to realize that however I combed my hair, it wasn't going to change my face, height, or build. And there was nothing special about these physical characteristics that would draw people to me.

I did notice, however, that some of the most popular kids at school also lacked the prototypical good looks of the pop singers on all the posters. What did they have? How did they do it? They just seemed to brim with confidence and charisma. They had an ability to make people laugh and didn't care what parents and teachers thought of them. I, on the other hand, was more on the shy and less confident side. I wanted to please my parents and teachers. I appreciated humor but of a sort that was not as appreciated by others. I certainly did not know how to "work a room" and charm people with an amazing personality. That was just not who I was.

The one area in which I tried my hardest to excel, however, was sports. Compared to some (especially when you include infants and the elderly), I had a bit of athletic ability. I could run fast and had some hand-eye coordination. What I lacked in stature I made up for in hustle and effort. Yet this did not lead to much success on the sports fields. I was cut four years in a row from our high school's varsity baseball team and started playing football during my senior year—too late to progress very far.

In all these ways, whether it be beauty, wealth, charisma, or talent, I could never distinguish myself among my peers. Rarely did people seek me out, ask my opinion, or invite me to events. And before I followed the Lord, these were the "shortcomings" that I most regretted. I also regretted my sin—my selfishness, lusts, lies, and laziness. I knew I did not measure up.

I did not feel special. And, in the world's eyes, I was not special—I did not stand out or rise above my peers in any way. I felt my presence was more of a nuisance to society than a benefit. Often, I felt that I just blended into the background—that no one saw me. It really would not have mattered if I were there or not. I had nothing to offer, no value to add, no worth to be wanted.

And then I wondered if God saw me. Did he notice my presence? Did he know I was here? Did he care? How could he? I was just one of billions of people in the world.

God told Abraham that his descendants would be as numerous as the stars in the sky. I often looked at the stars on summer nights. There were so many. A few of the bright ones stood out prominently. I knew I was not one of those stars. The bright stars composed constellations, and you could always quickly find them in the sky. I, however, felt like one of the millions of faint stars in between—hard to find and easily confused with others when searching for them. *Does God really know and care for all of them?*

Looking at the starlit sky on a summer night can make you feel quite small. I would think about the distances I was observing. Unfathomable. I would think of the sizes of the heavenly bodies—the earth, the sun, the moon, and the stars. How small are they in the vast expanse of space? And how small am I compared to them? I was just a speck of dust floating around on a bit bigger speck of dust in an endless universe that was mostly empty. My thoughts were not too different from the psalmist, who mused, "When I consider your heavens, the work of your fingers, the moon and the stars, which you have set in place, what is mankind that you are mindful of them, human beings that you care for them?" (Psalm 8:3-4 NIV).

When I was 17, I washed dishes at a steakhouse in town. After the last guest would rise from their table, I would wash their dishes and put them away before calling it a night. Some nights, when patrons lingered, the manager let the servers go home early and bussed the table himself. I had to stick around to clean up, however, and more than once the manager waited for me at the door, key in hand, ready to lock up as soon as I stepped out. Then, I would drive twenty minutes to our house out in the country, sometimes arriving home as late as 1:00 a.m. All was peaceful and quiet in the hills at this hour. My mom would leave a plate of food for me covered in the microwave.

One night when I arrived home late, the air was still and the sky was sparkling with an awe-inspiring display of stars. Incredibly majestic. Extremely quiet. A masterpiece sprawled out in the heavens above completely unnoticed and unappreciated by those who were sound asleep in their beds. But I saw it. I felt like I had a front row seat in an empty stadium about to watch the most amazing performance on stage. It was not to be missed.

Then a sense of smallness accompanied the awe I felt. Feelings of insignificance and worthlessness haunted me again. I felt inconsequential and unnecessary. Yet the majesty of the stars beckoned me to pray to their creator.

God?
Do you know I'm here?
Do you see me?
Do you care?

I kept looking at the same spot in the sky as I prayed. It was a group of three stars—an upside-down triangle. I was not praying to them, but for some reason I kept spying the triangle of stars as I prayed to God.

I was struggling to believe. I was contemplating whether I had any value. Then, as I prayed, I received an inaudible message. For the first time in my life, I felt God speak inside of my heart. Even though I was very confused, I knew it was him. He said to me, "Eliot, even though you don't understand everything now, there will come a day in the near future, when I will make you understand. Your confusion will disappear, and you will know."

I was very excited to hear this from God! Even though I was still confused and didn't know how everything worked, I felt God saying to me, "Have faith—a day is coming when you will understand."

I was so excited I asked God to show me a miracle to confirm that this voice was really from him. I wanted to be sure that it was not just my own idea but that it came from God. *Did I hear this message because it is what I wanted to hear? Was this "voice" just some sort of psychological trick my mind was playing on me?* So, I asked God for a miracle, a sign, to confirm that he spoke to me. I imagined a meteor dashing across the starry triangle that fixed my gaze. And this became my request—I asked God to shoot a meteor across the three stars, from right to left.

As soon as I prayed for this, a scripture came to mind. I remembered a verse that seemed to apply to my request. Jesus had said, "A wicked and adulterous generation asks for miraculous signs."

Oh! ... Oops.

My heart was immediately riddled with guilt. I promptly repented and prayed to God, "I'm so sorry!" I turned my back to the stars and continued my prayer, "God, I'm sorry for asking for a miraculous sign. I understand that you just want me to have faith that what you said to me was the truth. I don't need a miraculous sign; I will believe in you."

This is where God wanted me to be. I knew that to have faith in him was to trust him—to trust his voice speaking to me and to continue to walk in his way without requiring God to prove himself to me.

Okay. It was settled now. I was still happy for the peace that accompanied the promise of future resolution to my doubt and confusion. I resolved to continue to trust God and pursue him.

Before heading inside to sleep, I turned around and peeked at the three stars one more time. Then, in the space of a glance, a meteor streaked across the starry triangle! It shot from right to left and looked *exactly* as I had imagined it and asked God to show me.

Whoa!
A silent miracle.
A sign in the heavens.
A mercy for a young, vulnerable, yet sincere seeker of the Almighty.

At this moment, I knew I was in the presence of the Great. Chills ran through my body. Jesus saw me. I did not deserve the blessing of the sign he showed me, but he chose to grant it anyway.

When we become fully cognizant that we are presently in the hands of the Almighty, it is simultaneously amazing and terrifying. We have drawn the attention of the all-powerful God who sees right through us. Any pretense we have is exposed. Any hidden bias is obvious. Any secret sin is laid bare. We have no defense, no self-righteous claim to make. It is so terrifying we almost wished he had not noticed us at all. We wish he did not see us. Yet there is something completely wonderful about it too. The eyes that look upon us do so with mercy, kindness, and love. He has made us aware of his presence—not to smite us, but to call us; not to rebuke, but to redeem.

"Here I am Lord; send me!"

When we are redeemed by Jesus, when we are cleansed from our sin, and when we hear God's call, we are motivated to go. We will do whatever is asked.

It was two years later that I found Jesus during my freshman year of college. I was invited to attend the Bible study meeting of a campus ministry, and my world was turned upside down. Not only had I found true seekers and followers of Jesus, I began to get my questions answered by the campus minister, by the other students, and by looking at the Word of God together with them. God's words to me—that one day I would come to understand—came true. God kept his promise to me. Then on March 28, 1990, I was baptized by my campus minister in the salty waves of the Atlantic Ocean. I was ready to serve God in any way he asked.

Seven years later, I found myself in Laos. I was there for the summer. I still did not yet feel called there, but after considering many options, it was where God had drawn my heart and attention.

One afternoon I pedaled my bicycle down the tree-lined Kuvieng Road on my way to teach English at the Ministry of Finance in Vientiane, the capital city of Laos. This road took me by a squatter village, a fresh market, and the bus station. As I rode past a sandlot next to the squatter village, a group of young boys was playing a pickup game of soccer. I glanced their way and noticed one of the young boys plant his foot to kick the ball. When he did, however, he slipped and fell headlong to the ground. He responded with a sheepish smile, and the entire group erupted in laughter. It was a simple and sweet moment. I imagined Jesus kicking around in the sand with them, making them laugh. It reminded me of the Sandi Patty song, often sung at weddings back in the early 90s, "Love Will Be Our Home" about being able to live wherever there is love, children laughing and people singing.

As I cycled past, I noticed the pushcart vendors along the street. Ladies sold grilled sticks of meat, fish, and other "to go" food. Some of them pounded slivers of green papaya in large clay mortar and pestle pots. They wore printed wrap skirts and red cloth aprons and had their hair tied back in ponytails. Most of them had straight faces and seemed tired and weary. I then imagined Jesus walking along the road, chatting with them and getting them to smile through simple conversation and kindness. With a few words, he would summon laughter. I envisioned faces of stone melting to radiate joy.

These visions prompted me to pray. "Lord, I want to be like that! I want to play with kids in the sand! I want to turn people's lives of drudgery to joy. I want to make the hardest people soften and the saddest person smile. Lord, I want to be like Jesus for the Lao people!" It was at this moment that I felt Laos was where the Lord wanted me to serve. He had given me a vision of the joy and laughter I could help bring to Lao people's lives.

I was elated. My heart pounded and adrenaline pumped through my body. I found myself pedaling faster. I reached the end of the street where Kuvieng

Road intersects with Lane Xang Avenue—the main drag through Vientiane city. I turned right onto Lane Xang. In the distance was the conspicuous form of the Victory Gate Monument. I would ride my bike past this monument before reaching my destination. My mind was still on the vision of Jesus in the market and my heart was still pumping.

As I approached the towering Victory Gate, God gave me another vision of Jesus. This time it was an image of Jesus, covered in blood, suffering and dying on the cross. Nails were piercing the flesh of his hands and feet. Streaks of sweat and blood caked his face and skin. Flies swarmed at his side where the soldiers had pierced him. His head hung limp, adorned with a crown of thorns.

Then I heard God speak to my heart again. He said, "So, you want to be like me?"

The point was not lost on me. If I was going to be like Jesus for the Lao people, was I willing to suffer and die for them too?

SECOND CONVERSION

I never knew air could be so muggy and thick with humidity. My friend Kaosing and I just finished playing basketball at an open-air gym in Vientiane. We played hard and sweated buckets. The humidity did not help. We were dehydrated and eager to hop on the motorbike to get the wind blowing. However, because of the extreme heat, even speeding on the motorbike did not really help. It just felt like a giant blast of hot air.

We whizzed down Kuvieng Road—a street that followed the old wall and moat around the ancient city. Large trees lined the roadway and provided staggered bits of shade along the route home. It was so hot that even the pavement was melting. A good sharp turn with rubber tires smeared the softened asphalt.

Kuvieng Road was my favorite route to take on hot days. Even though the sky was blue and there was no sign of rain, I could have sworn that I felt drops of water falling upon me as I drove under the trees.

The trees reminded me of my first trip to Laos in 1997. I was with Austin, a seasoned missionary who later invited me to join his team, and his daughter who stayed in an apartment near the Mekong River in downtown Vientiane. Austin wanted to go swimming in the river one evening, so we cut through a Buddhist temple on our way to the water's edge. As we walked through the courtyard, all of a sudden we were immersed in an extraordinary fragrance. Austin immediately halted and pointed out the flowering Dok Champa tree (plumeria) responsible for the sweet smell. It was amazing to me—I was in an enchanted tropical paradise of aromatic flowering trees.

The dripping trees along Kuvieng Road reminded me of the Dok Champa experience from years before. The drops of nectar from these trees provided me with the slightest sensation of coolness on the hottest days. I imagined the water to be a naturally fragrant perfume, though I could not detect an aroma.

They were like "blessing trees," I fantasized, providing a respite from the scorching sun and dripping with morsels of refreshment for the weary traveler who took refuge under their limbs.

As Kaosing and I returned home from basketball, I again felt the drops of water. I asked him if he felt them too.

"Yes, I do," he replied with an ever eager and positive attitude.

"Do you know what that is? Is it the tree's sap or nectar from flowers?" I queried.

"No. It is a type of insect. This insect always likes to live in this kind of tree. The water you feel is the insect urinating on you!"

Oh!

I was jolted from my romantic interpretation. Kaosing had said it so matter of factly, as if it didn't bother him at all. But it definitely took the whole "enchanted trees of blessing" feeling right out of the experience for me!

Kaosing was a good companion. Even though he was only fifteen and I was thirty, we had a good friendship. Kaosing was from the Mien tribe—the same unreached people group I wanted to target—and as a new believer, he allowed me to disciple him. We spent a lot of time together, and I learned much about Laos from him as I dedicated my first year in the country to language study.

One experience with Kaosing became a seminal moment for me. I had many of those my first year. I was telling him a story about a tourist I had seen in the city. The tourist had done something I deemed insensitive to the local culture, and I was embarrassed for all expatriates. I made a comment about how Lao people are exceedingly more polite than foreigners are.

My last statement elicited a facial response from Kaosing I rarely witnessed. It was clear he did not agree. He still did not say anything, however. Normally, a Lao person would not reveal their disagreement with someone who is older than they are. It is a way to maintain respect and honor the "face" of the elder. But I immediately recognized a learning opportunity for me.

"You don't agree?" I asked him rather directly. Kaosing was Mien and a little more accustomed to directness than Lao people are, though I did not understand that at the time. "How do you see things?"

"I think foreigners are more polite than Lao people," he answered.

What? I thought. *Not even close, in my book.* He was obviously seeing things differently than me and I wanted to understand.

"Why do you think that?" I investigated.

Kaosing thought for a moment and finally responded, "Well, I think Lao people are polite to foreigners. But to other Lao people, especially young people, they are not very polite."

Wow. Kaosing had just given me another perspective. It was a perspective I coveted. However, it was one of which I was unaware. I had judged Lao people in the same way most people judge others—based upon how they treated *me*. I never noticed any difference. I had just assumed that because Lao people treated me so politely they must treat all people politely too. But Kaosing opened my eyes to perhaps the most important social dynamic in Lao culture—a dynamic that many outsiders never truly come to understand: social hierarchy.

Social hierarchy in Lao society is not simply a class or caste system. To be sure, social class plays a part, but the hierarchy exists within all classes and communities. In fact, it emerges in every single relationship between any two people.

On another occasion, I was telling Kaosing a story about a campus minister friend of mine. I called him my friend because I didn't know a better word to use in the Lao language. I told Kaosing how this man had memorized the entire New Testament. Later, when it came out that this man was almost seventy years old, Kaosing laughed and told me that the man was not my friend. I was confused. He was not my relative, boss, colleague, or neighbor. He was just a man I knew, we were on good terms, and so I called him my friend. He was certainly not my enemy! Nevertheless, Kaosing explained to me that someone who is forty years older could not be my friend. Clearly, the word I kept using did not mean what I thought it meant.

The word in Lao that we often translate "friend" actually refers to one's peer and companion. To me, "friend" meant someone unrelated and with whom I had a good-standing relationship. However, the term in Lao refers to someone who is of the same social status—a status that is primarily defined by relative age. Someone who is forty years my senior is much higher in the social hierarchy than me and is on the level of father, not friend. In my world, I would only call someone "father" who is biologically related to me or who has adopted me as his son. In Laos anyone who is in the same age range as your father is commonly called "father," even though you have no blood relation.

Years later, when my wife, Mali (who is Lao), met my parents and immediately started calling them "Mom" and "Dad," they were touched. For Americans, to have a daughter-in-law call you these familial terms feels like she has accepted you as loving surrogate parents. When not already related by blood, the terms refer to the good quality of the relationship. For Lao people, however, the terms "mom" and "dad" simply refer to one's status in the social hierarchy. Because of the relative age of my parents to Mali, calling them "Mom" and "Dad" was the only polite choice she had. (Sorry, Mom and Dad—she really does love you!)

In countless ways Lao culture is on the opposite end of the spectrum from Western cultures. In America, we highly value the concept of equality. We have never had a king, royal family, or system of nobility in our society. The thought of having a monarch rule over us immediately elicits a visceral reaction against the idea. To have any sort of hierarchy implies arrogance, pride, corruption, and the like. Lao people, however, certainly recognize the vices of pride and corruption but do not consider their cause to be the absence of social equality.

In English, we use the same set of pronouns for all people with whom we speak, whether they are children, friends, the elderly, or God. "You" can apply to anyone, and "I" always applies to ourselves when we speak with any of these different parties. In the Lao language, this is not the case. There are no true generic pronouns to use with anyone and everyone. If you speak with someone a bit younger, you call them *nong* (younger sibling) and yourself *ai* or *eauay* (older brother or older sister). When you speak to someone your parent's age, you call them *mae* (mother) or *paw* (father) and yourself *louk* (child). To use the more generic term *chao* (you) for someone your parent's age is somewhat disrespectful. To use that same term (*chao*) with an intruder or thief would be showing too much respect. Furthermore, when talking to high-ranking government officials, respected religious leaders, or decorated professors, you would use a completely different set of pronouns for these formal relationships. Finally, when worshiping God, one uses yet another set of pronouns to properly represent the ultimate respect shown to the Almighty.

It took me a long time to understand the implications of all these dynamics. Without learning the language, making friends with Lao people who were unfamiliar with Western culture, and immersing myself into Lao culture, I never would have begun to understand Lao people in the way that Lao people understand themselves and understand the world. When I progressed in the language enough to have deeper conversations with Lao people, I realized that they were much different than I had once assumed. Previously, all I knew about Lao people was what I read or what other expatriates had told me about them. After learning the language to the point I could have deeper relationships with them, my ideas about Lao people changed significantly. A great deal of what I had heard and assumed was off target. Some of it was partially true but not nuanced. I discovered that much of the misunderstanding we Westerners had about Lao people, good or bad, was due to projection.

I will never forget when I was once the victim of projection. It happened innocently enough with a respected Lao pastor named Nokeo in a Lao campus ministry service. Nokeo was a young and talented man who was well rooted in the Bible. Once a non-believing student himself, another Lao Christian reached out to Nokeo by giving him a Bible. Nokeo was not interested in reading it, however. Instead, he found that the thin pages were perfect for rolling up bootleg tobacco for homemade cigarettes. In fact, Nokeo smoked the entire Bible before he ever read it. After he smoked the last page, he returned to his Christian friend to ask him for another Bible. This time, however, he read it and the Holy Spirit grabbed his heart. Nokeo began serving the Lord and making disciples of other university students.

By this time, Nokeo had been working in campus ministry for many years and led a group of about forty or more Lao university students. It was their Sunday morning service and I attended with a friend. I was the only non-Lao person there. Nokeo strode back and forth in the room as he taught. His style was very effective at communicating with students in a way that made them think, consider, and develop their faith. This style was in contrast to that of many pastors who simply preached homilies while the audience waited patiently for it to be finished, looking at their phones or whispering to their neighbors to pass the time. Nokeo's style was more dynamic, and he was challenging them to live a life fully committed to trusting the Lord.

I understood his words and agreed with his message. Then it happened. Nokeo walked toward me and pointed me out to the crowd. As the only white person in the room, I was an easy target. He did not ask me a question or prompt me to share anything with the group. Instead, I became a sermon illustration. Nokeo explained to his listeners that as an American I really understood what it meant to live a life fully committed to Jesus Christ. I do not remember what he said verbatim, but I definitely remember the gist of his words: "American Christians really 'get it,' unlike we Lao Christians who only dabble around with our faith." I was the prop for his challenge to the Lao students. As they listened, they nodded in agreement. What Nokeo had said made complete sense to them.

Whoa! Wait, wait, wait! Don't they have this completely turned around? Aren't Lao Christians more committed? Isn't their faith more authentic than our Western version? I had heard many stories of Lao people walking through jungles and over mountains for days just to attend secret Bible trainings. There were stories of Lao believers who were arrested, persecuted, and killed just for refusing to recant their faith in Christ. I had heard that the Lao government wanted to rid the entire country of Christianity, which they had branded the religion of the enemy. The church persisted in this country only because of an extreme and authentic faith in the hearts of Lao believers. They would not back down on their convictions, no matter the cost. In fact, I had once seen a video produced by a group of short-term missionaries to Laos proclaiming that "there are no lukewarm Christians in Laos." *If this is the case, what could Pastor Nokeo possibly see in me? And why are all the Lao students nodding?*

I had just become the object of his projection. And while it completely embarrassed me in the moment, it taught me a great lesson. As believable as Pastor Nokeo's projection of a "super-faith" on me was to his listeners, it was not really the case. I trust that my faith is authentic and I am committed to Christ, but Pastor Nokeo did not know me well enough to observe this for himself. Instead, he was assuming it based upon my identity markers. Certainly, those of us in the West would not boast of a "super-faith" possessed by the majority of Western and American Christians.

The lesson this experience taught me, however, is that I had been just as guilty of projecting a "super-faith" on Lao Christians. In fact, as I searched my heart and reviewed previous statements I had made to others at home while trying to motivate them to be all in with missions and Jesus, I realized that I had long projected an image of authentic Christianity on non-Western believers, especially those from undeveloped nations. I was not particularly impressed with my own culture's version of Christianity and the level of commitment to

Jesus found therein, and I often found it a useful tool to tell fellow Americans how Christians on the other side of the world really get it and live their lives fully committed to Jesus. I remembered how most times I taught like this, American Christians readily agreed with me that the non-Western church was not as lazy, materialistic, and distracted as we were. Now Pastor Nokeo was using this exact same tactic with his disciples.

After this incident, I realized just how prevalent projection is, especially in cross-cultural situations. I began to notice it everywhere.

I overheard a European backpacker tell another traveler how he visited a temple and "got blessed" by a Buddhist monk. The other replied how cool that was. I wondered if they would have thought it as "cool" to visit a church in their home country and be prayed for by a bishop. Were they projecting a level of spiritual authenticity upon the Buddhist monk they would not afford a Christian clergy member? I can only suspect.

A female tourist sat cross-legged in front of a young novice monk and quizzed him on Buddhist beliefs and spirituality. His highly accented English lent an air of wisdom to his words. She was clearly impressed. Unbeknownst to her, in Lao, he and his monk friends giggled about this attractive young woman paying him so much attention. While she saw their interaction as spiritual learning, the monks saw it as flirting.

An American visitor rode in my truck through the countryside of Laos and shook her head at the level of poverty she witnessed. She felt it was a shame that people lived like that. Then she quipped, "But they are just so content with what they have." I gently challenged her, "You have been here for a few days now. What do you see that convinces you the people are content?" Slightly taken aback, she asked honestly, "Well, aren't they content with what they have?" I explained that I did not know of any person in the country of Laos, who lived in a bamboo and thatch-roofed house, who did not wish to upgrade. If they had the means to do so, they would immediately build brick-and-mortar houses with tiled roofs and air-conditioning. Somehow, she had interpreted their friendliness and hospitality as contentment with their own level of poverty. I well remember projecting the same thing upon Haitian believers when I returned to the States from a trip there in 1991. "They don't have anything, but they are so content!" It was another way for me to challenge American Christians to give up their luxuries and live for Jesus.

A daring group of short-term Bible smugglers arrived to help us move some materials. I had met their leader on a previous visit he made, and now he was leading others who came for the first time. As we finished our meal, his team asked him how much of a tip they should leave.

"Oh, tipping is not customary in Asia," he explained. "They are a very service-oriented culture. In fact, if you tip them, they will be offended."

The truth is, while tipping is not customary, it is certainly not offensive. My friend was intending to compliment the culture, but he was projecting a misinterpretation.

Another group of visitors traveled to a northern province where they met a local Christian. He was friendly toward them and took them around. Later, they reported they had met a trustworthy local believer. I quizzed them about this man and how they had determined he was trustworthy. "Well, he is a Christian—he smiled a lot and just seemed genuine" was the answer. Later, I learned that this man and his father had embezzled large chunks of money from other unsuspecting Christian tourists.

My young Lao friends in the remote province of Bokeo loved to watch Western movies. They visited my house one night and asked, "Eliot, can we watch a movie where they ride horses?" I put on a DVD of *Dances with Wolves* and did my best to translate the events and dialogue into Lao. They were very patient with me and watched the story develop with rapt attention. Of special delight to them was the scene when Kevin Costner's character, John Dunbar, first meets the native Lakota men. He jumps around like a four-legged animal to learn the Lakota word for buffalo—*tatanka*. They sit and watch him grind coffee, and they taste sugar for the first time. The young Lao men giggled watching these interactions. After a while, it dawned on me that my Lao friends identified with John Dunbar more than the Lakota natives. This surprised me.

Why did it surprise me? I had assumed the opposite because as Asians their skin and hair more closely matched that of the Native Americans. John Dunbar was a white American like me. Most anthropologists would regard Lao culture as being on the opposite end of the spectrum from American culture. My

Lao friends' cross-cultural relationship with me matched the Lakota natives' relationship with John Dunbar, I reasoned. Consequently, I had presumed they would identify more with the Lakota Native Americans.

However, the young Lao men did not see it this way. In their minds, John Dunbar came from a more technologically advanced society than that of the Lakota men. The discrepancy that stood out to them was not that of skin color, language, and worldview. Instead, it was technology. The level of technological advancement in the Lakota society was far below that of both John Dunbar's and of my Lao friends. In fact, these young Lao men were living in a village that had recently gotten electricity. We had cell phone service, televisions, motorcycles, and electric fans. Consequently, they viewed themselves as technologically superior to the Lakota natives and even to John Dunbar. From their point of view, the Lakota men were as different from them as the Lakota men would have been different from me. As the more advanced character in the movie's portrayal, my Lao friends could relate to John Dunbar.

These experiences initiated a series of paradigm shifts that transformed my perspective. I realized that I had been projecting in both negative and positive ways on Lao people. On one hand, I had assumed someone was honest because they smiled. I assumed they were spiritual when they spoke with an accent. I assumed something exotic was somehow more authentic. The grass just seemed greener on the other side of the world.

On the other hand, I had initially interpreted the Lao social hierarchy and demand for respect to be born out of pride and arrogance. I assumed their reluctance to reveal vulnerability as an inappropriate repression of emotion. I misinterpreted Lao men's embarrassment to show public affection to their wives as a lack of love for them. Furthermore, I assumed that my Western culture and English language were "normal" and the standard from which all others varied. It struck me one day that English was just as much a random and arbitrary language as was Lao.

It was time to wipe my slate clean and grow to know Lao people as they knew themselves.

To be certain, I do not consider myself to have arrived. It will take a lifetime of immersion to begin to approach deep understanding. But the distance I have already come has been like a second conversion for me.

My life was forever transformed when I turned to Christ. Nothing will ever compare to that level of total transformation. Everything scripture says about being "born again," the old self dying and becoming a new creation, applied to me. Repentance, as I experienced it, was not just being contrite for my shortcomings but completely reorienting my life. Repentance does not mean "sorry" so much as it means "turn." In the vernacular of the early 90s: do a 180. No longer do we live for ourselves, as Paul says in 2 Corinthians 5, but we live for him who died for us and rose again. We do not serve our own purposes; we serve his—eagerly and gladly!

To a lesser extent, living immersed in Lao society also transformed my life. I changed. I am not the same man who moved to Laos less than two months after the September 11 terrorist attacks in New York and Washington. I became something new, something different. It's difficult to explain to someone who has not experienced it. I do not claim to have "gone native" or "become Lao." But I have learned to see the world from an entirely different perspective. I think I have become what some describe as a "Third Culture Kid," though I am not a kid. I can understand and operate fully in both places and in both societies. But I am no longer a good fit in either one. Each side sees me as belonging to the other.

I am blessed to have three wonderful and beautiful children. Both Lao and American people love to comment on who takes after whom. I have found the general consensus to be quite fascinating. With few exceptions, Americans say that my children take after Mali. Lao people, on the other hand, usually say they look like me. Both tend to notice the features of the other race more readily in my children and match them to the parent responsible.

In some ways, that is how I feel as a "third culture person." Most people more quickly recognize the traits in me that are different and match me to the culture responsible. But for what purpose did God lead me to become this "third culture person"?

By the way, sometimes, this works in the opposite direction too. When my daughter was about five years old, we visited my parents in the States. As we drove out of their driveway one day, my kids noticed a large fluffy gray squirrel run across their front yard. My daughter exclaimed, "Look—a squirrel! It's so cute! Shoot it!" We all laughed. Now, when I tell this story at home, Americans will say, "Yep! She's from the Ozarks!" When I tell this story in Laos, they say, "She's definitely Lao!" In this case, a commonality can be a bridge. I suppose both Midwestern hillbillies and Lao people like to kill and eat cute, furry wildlife.

The Lord often leads us down paths we do not understand. A faithful disciple does not need to understand. All he needs to do is keep his eyes on Jesus and follow in his footsteps. Though we would like to see the entire path mapped out ahead, and may even desire to determine the route ourselves, following Jesus step by step requires both faith and attention. We must have faith to trust him to decide where he will take us. We must pay attention so that we do not lose him, especially when he makes a quick turn.

When I first went to Laos, I told people that I would not marry a Lao girl. I was never theologically against the idea. I just thought I would be able to understand and trust another American at a level I could never approach with someone from a different culture. As I learned the Lao language, however, and as I experienced the transformation described above, my feelings began to change. I found myself imagining my future married to a Lao girl. At first, it startled me, and I tried to reject the notion. But as I continued to immerse myself in Lao society, it started to make more sense. Finally, in prayer, I felt God leading me in that direction. This was long before I met Mali or knew who she was.

God was leading me down a path I never would have predicted or chosen for myself. I believe God does this with us because he wants to prepare us for greater things ahead—things he will lead us to do that we never would have imagined or volunteered to do on our own. In Acts 9, Jesus chose Paul to be his "chosen instrument" to reach the Gentiles. Yet, before Paul would complete that task, Jesus said that he would show him "how much he must suffer for my name."

I never knew that I would experience what I describe as a "second conversion" in Laos or that I would become a "third culture person." I never could have predicted that my perspective would have changed so greatly. Yet God knew all along. He wanted me to understand the itch people felt so that I could best be in a position to scratch it. He led me to this point in order to prepare me for the next chapter of what he planned to do.

Little was I aware, however, of all the adventures that awaited.

4

THE MIEN

BOKEO

"Wait! Wait! We're coming too!" the Mien ladies shouted as they scurried down the hill to the street where my truck was stopped. They scrambled toward my truck with anxious vigor. I pressed the brake to the floor as they climbed into the back. "Thank you!" they said, catching their breath. "Okay, we're all in. Go, go!" Someone tapped the roof of the cab twice to indicate I could proceed.

The bed of my truck was now filled with Mien families. Most of them sat on the twin rows of benches under the roof-topper affixed to the back of my Toyota pickup. Some of them squatted in the middle, bracing themselves on the knees of others. A couple of the men stood on the back bumper and held on to a vertical bar welded to the topper for just that purpose.

We were headed to Nakam village. It was about 40 minutes up in the mountains from town. We had planted a new church there, and the Mien believers bubbled with smiles and laughter as they prepared to worship together. Many of the Mien living in town hailed from Nakam and wanted to catch the free ride up to Sunday services in their home village. I made the rounds in town that morning picking up multiple families to accompany us. The younger ones rarely had the opportunity to ride in the back of a pickup truck. They sang joyfully as the truck bounced along the bumpy dirt road, crossing ditches and navigating log bridges over mountain streams. I smiled at the sound of their singing and thought to myself, *There is nowhere else I'd rather be.*

Finally, we arrived in the village, and I parked my truck next to the new church building. It was still yellow from the fresh hand-hewn boards and newly assembled thatch roof. As the Mien people spilled out of the truck, Pastor Tsoi noticed me walking off toward the bushes. I needed to relieve myself discreetly before joining the worship service.

He inquired, "Where are you going?"

"I'm going to shoot a rabbit," I replied.

"Shoot a rabbit," or *nying gatai* in Lao, is a euphemism for urination. Lao people use this term for traveling situations when one must "do their business" in the woods or bushes along the road. Only men "shoot rabbits." Women, on the other hand, "pick flowers" (*gep dok mai*).

Not all Lao people are familiar with this euphemism, especially not ethnic minority children who only began learning to speak Lao when they enrolled in school a few years before. This became evident when two of the young Mien girls heard that I was going to shoot a rabbit and saw me approaching the woods. They immediately started to follow and said they would help "grab it" for me.

I told them it would not be necessary. Pastor Tsoi got a good laugh. So did the Mien girls when he explained the meaning to them.

Pastor Tsoi was the first believer in Nakam Village. Like many people in Laos, he was bilingual, speaking both his native Mien language and the *lingua franca* Lao of the majority people, as well. Lao is very similar to Thai, so many Lao people enjoy Thai television and radio programs. Pastor Tsoi first heard the gospel himself through a Thai Christian radio broadcast. As he listened, his heart was compelled to believe. But Tsoi didn't know what to do. How could he become a Christian? He had never met a Christian before and assumed there were no Christians in Laos. Consequently, Tsoi traveled to Chiang Rai, Thailand, to find a church. There he met a pastor who led him to faith and baptized him. He returned home full of joy and excitement about sharing the transformative nature of Christ's good news with his fellow villagers.

Tsoi's excitement soon met opposition. Once his father heard the news of his faith, he disowned Tsoi. He told him that he was no longer his son because he turned his back on his family's spirits. As animists, Mien people believe that each household has spirits—these include both spirits of the house, village, nature, and ancestral spirits as well. When a man dies, his children must "feed" his spirit through regular offerings and rituals. Usually this is the responsibility of the oldest son. If a spirit is not fed, it can become angry or evil. Mien parents feel supremely dishonored if they learn their children will refuse to feed their spirits after they die. It is akin to condemning them to hell.

Tsoi remained faithful to the Lord. He led his grandmother to faith and his wife and children. Then, one Sunday morning, Tsoi showed up at the feed mill in Bokeo where I raised chickens. He had heard there were Christians at our company and wanted to investigate. When my teammates encountered a Mien man inquiring about Christians, they directed him to me. They knew I would be interested in talking to a new Mien believer.

My heart was set on reaching the Mien people. They were the group I had picked off a list of unreached peoples in Laos years before my first visit. At the time, the Joshua Project published a list of 1,739 unreached people groups left in the world and recorded 32 groups for Laos. The Highland Yao (Mien) were one of the larger groups, and they are located in the north. We had contacts with missionaries in the north (where I eventually went to work in Bokeo) and thought the Mien would be a good choice.

The Mien are an ethnic minority in Laos, similar to the Hmong. They are animists, unlike the predominant *Lao Loum* (Lowland Lao) majority people who are Buddhist. As animists, they rely upon shamans to perform spiritual rituals to appease malevolent spirits who might harm them and to placate ancestral and common spirits in order to obtain health and wealth. The Mien inhabit the areas of Laos near the borders of Thailand, China, and Vietnam—countries also possessing Mien communities. When I first arrived in Laos, the Mien were less than 1% Christian. However, Christianity had been in Laos long before my first visit in 1997.

The first protestant missionary to visit Laos, Daniel McGilvary, famously rode elephants from Chiang Mai, Thailand, to the royal city of Luang Prabang, the capital of *Laan Xang*—the Kingdom of a Million Elephants—in 1885. Later, around the turn of the century, Swiss missionaries established a beachhead in southern Laos by converting those who were possessed by demons. In the late 1940s, the Christian and Missionary Alliance (CMA) established the largest network of churches and Bible schools in Laos. The remnants of the CMA work later became the government-authorized Lao Evangelical Church (LEC). When communist influence first creeped into northern Laos, a CMA family saw God move among the Hmong people when a shaman (spirit priest) became a follower of Christ and led many others to faith. In more recent times, God has moved among the Khmu people. The Khmu have seen many of their own endure long and cruel prison sentences, but they likely boast the largest number of Christians in Laos.

Christian missionaries had been in and out of Laos for more than a century by the time I first stepped foot on Lao soil. After the Communist Revolution in the mid-1970s, the Lao church was forced to stand on its own and has done so successfully in terms of leadership, if not in finances. Since the early 1990s, when Laos began to open up, the church has steadily grown. A decade later, the LEC had three main churches in Vientiane Capital conducting weekly public services. During my first year in the capital, I spent most Sunday mornings sitting cross-legged on the floor of the Anou church, trying my best to understand the Lao pastor's sermon.

Bokeo province was different. There was no official LEC church in the provincial capital of Huay Xai when I lived there. There were a few Khmu and Hmong churches in the district but none among the Mien. Nakam was the closest Mien village to the city, and before Tsoi believed, there were no Christians there.

I was familiar with Nakam village. We had an effective excuse for visiting and secretly prayer-walking through the village. To be precise, I should probably describe it as prayer-*riding*.

Nakam had elephants—two of them. One of the villagers had purchased them for logging. He took the elephants out to the virgin forest on the edge of the village, attached giant logs to their harnesses, and drove them back home with shouts and cracks of his bamboo whip. They were aged and frail animals, probably sold off at the end of their days for a good price. Rings of long heavy chains encompassed their necks. Large bones readily protruded beneath their thick and lean hides.

The owner was happy when visitors came to ride his elephants. For a few dollars, we would ride them for more than an hour. He made more money hosting these rides than he could from logging, and it was much easier on the animals. Without any ladders or saddles, we climbed the lifted leg of the elephant and sat on its neck grasping the chains. Its shoulders rocked us back and forth as it walked, and its ears flapped against our legs. As it lumbered from the south side to the north end of the village and back, we prayed over the entire village. "Lord, may your good news open the eyes and hearts of these people! May they turn to you and know your love." Later, around a short table in the village headman's house, we prayed a prayer of blessing upon him, the food, and the village.

Little did we know how God was going to answer our prayers.

———————

"He said if he ever saw me visit their house again, he would kill both her and me!" Chai told us with concern.

It was the first time I had met Chai, Pastor Tsoi's wife. Chai did not speak much Lao, but it was enough for my partner and me to understand. It had been a week since I had met Pastor Tsoi and I had not heard from him again. Nakam village did not have cell phone coverage, and Pastor Tsoi did not own a phone. We decided just to drive up to the village and pay him a visit.

Pastor Tsoi was not at home. His wife, Chai, was surprised to see us. She had just believed in Christ a few weeks before but was already actively sharing her faith with her neighbors. Immediately, she took us around to visit a number of the villagers with whom she had been sharing. Some of them were sick, and some of them were just curious about this new faith. We prayed for each one as we made our way to the edge of the northern village.

Suddenly, Chai stopped and turned to us with a serious look. "Do you see that house over there?" She pointed to a thatched roof bamboo house, nearly identical to most every other house in Nakam North. "We can't go over there, but we can stand here and pray for that family. I shared the gospel with the wife and she believed! But her husband threatened to kill her. He is angry with me too. He said if he ever saw me visit their house again, he would kill both her and me!"

Pray we did. This was a spiritual battle. The threat of death was a new experience for this Christian woman, so young in her faith. We did not want to see Satan squelch a meager beachhead in Nakam village. So, we prayed for the husband and his newly believing wife and for Chai too. As we prayed, the woman who had just believed, Nailin, noticed us from a distance and headed our way. She was very pregnant, and her face wore an expression of concern. We prayed for her too.

Countless times I have prayed because it seemed like the appropriate thing to do. Sometimes, it was just because I did not know what else to do. Christians pray—that is our normal practice—so I did too. To be certain, I believed that God could answer our prayers and do a miracle, but I was not sure if I could expect him to perform one for real.

The following Sunday morning after visiting Nakam village and praying for Nailin, I joined with the other missionaries at the house on the company grounds for English-language worship. We were in the habit of fellowshipping together, when everyone was in town, rather than joining any of the underground house churches. The presence of a foreigner at a small village church meeting would draw too much attention. Therefore, two other families and I met to worship, read the Bible, discuss its meaning, take communion, and pray.

Before we finished our simple service, an old Jeep rolled through our front gate. We heard the commotion and ran outside to see what was happening. It was the pregnant woman from Nakam, Nailin, who had just believed in Jesus. She was half-conscious in the back of the Jeep, accompanied by a small group of new Mien believers who brought her down the mountain. She had given birth and was losing blood. They wanted our help to save her life.

Early that morning, while it was still dark, Nailin walked out of the house and into the edge of the woods to "pick flowers." As she squatted, the time arrived for her baby to be born. Labor was short. In a few moments, she gave birth to a baby girl. Without any assistance, however, the placenta was not completely expelled, and she began to bleed profusely. With all her strength, she clutched her newborn and made her way back to her house. She collapsed in the doorway and lost consciousness.

Nailin's husband was at home and was startled to hear the new baby crying. But even the cries of a newborn did not soften his heart. Still angry about Nailin's decision to follow Jesus, he decided to let both her and the baby die where they lay. He did not lift a finger to help them.

Later that morning word made it to Chai that Nailin had given birth and was in trouble. Chai knew she must act fast and hired a man with the only vehicle in the village—an old Jeep—to take them down the mountain. The Jeep owner was hesitant to drive into town, since his vehicle was not licensed. "Just take us to the company, and Eliot will help us," Chai demanded.

"Put her in Eliot's truck!" my colleague Austin commanded when they arrived at the company. "You want to do ministry with Mien people, well here's your chance." I was eager to serve but unsure of what to do. This was my first time to assist in a medical emergency. The Mien people wanted to take her across the Mekong River to a hospital in Thailand, but I knew that would cost too much time with the paperwork hassle. I decided to take them to the

Lao hospital in Huay Xai.

I backed my truck up to the front door while the Mien brothers and sisters shouted to hospital staff to come fetch Nailin quickly. Someone handed me her baby, wrapped in a dirty cloth. She had not been bathed since her birth, and the umbilical cord was still attached. It was my first time to hold a newborn. She seemed healthy, but I didn't know anything about babies. Then, when the hospital staff saw me holding the baby, they assumed I was the father!

The doctors removed the rest of the placenta from Nailin's uterus and stopped the bleeding. Later, one of the other missionaries donated his blood to replace what she had lost. Nailin was still in a lot of pain, but she was going to survive. We were relieved but still felt sorry for her.

We stood around Nailin as she writhed in pain on the cold stainless steel table in the hospital. She kept muttering something in the Mien language which I could not understand. I assumed she was cursing God, life, or her husband, who did not even accompany her down the mountain to the hospital. I inquired about what she was saying, and they answered me in Lao, "She is praising God! She is saying that if it weren't for God, she would be dead already!" *Wow.* I was impressed with her faith!

However, I was not impressed with her husband. As we stood around Nailin and prayed for her, we also prayed that God would somehow break through to her husband's heart and turn him toward God and his wife.

Then, a few days later, it happened. Nailin's husband's legs swelled up for no known reason. They became so swollen he could not walk. He did not know what to do. Normally, when a Mien person has a physical ailment, they call in the shaman, or spirit doctor, to perform a ceremony to placate the afflicting spirit and heal the sickness. Shamans do not work for free, however, and Nailin's husband did not have either the money or the animal required for the sacrifice. The new Mien believers begged him to allow them to pray for him. Finally, when he felt he was at the end of his rope and knew no other way, he acquiesced. The believers laid their hands on him and asked God to heal his legs.

Over the next few days, to his surprise, Nailin's husband's legs improved greatly. So much so that he could walk again. The miracle melted his heart of stone, and he, too, put his faith in Jesus.

The following week, I joined the growing group of Mien Christians on Sunday morning for worship. This morning, we met in Nailin's house, the same one we would not venture to approach previously. Pastor Tsoi was there and spoke boldly, "That's right! Just a few weeks ago, this was a house divided. The husband refused to talk with his wife. They would not even eat food out of the same pot! But what Satan once separated, God has now brought together!"

Nailin handed me her baby and asked me to pray for her. I asked if they had named her and they told me it was a name from the Bible. They tested my Bible knowledge by saying, "She is named after King David's youngest daughter!" I paused to think about it—I didn't know the name of David's youngest daughter but only that his oldest daughter was named Tamar. I said aloud that Tamar was the only daughter I could remember David having. Then I mentioned the names of his three most prominent wives: Michal, Abigail, and Bathsheba.

"Michal was not David's daughter?" Pastor Tsoi asked sheepishly. He had read that she was the daughter of the king but had confused King David and King Saul. Michal was the youngest daughter of King Saul and became David's first wife. "That's okay," I said, "Michal is a beautiful name!" I did not want to embarrass Pastor Tsoi but rejoice in God's new gift to this family and the community of believers.

Baby Michal became the miraculous sign for the budding Nakam church. She was a sign that God was real, that in Christ we can overcome, and that the Lord takes care of his children.

The number of Mien believers was growing. After discussing it with Pastor Tsoi, he agreed that the new believers should be baptized. The Mien brothers and sisters dammed up a mountain stream high in the jungle above the village in order to create a pool large enough for immersion. Pastor Tsoi was the only one who had ever been baptized or seen a baptism. He had never baptized anyone. So, I baptized the first few as an example and then told him he must baptize the rest. Altogether, fourteen Mien people were baptized on the mountain that day.

Nailin's husband, whose legs were healed but still weak, chose not to climb the steep and slippery rocks along the mountain stream. Instead, he waited in the village. When we returned, Pastor Tsoi baptized him in a small fishpond next to one of the houses. It was the first time in the history of the world that someone was baptized into Christ in Nakam village.

During 2003, we saw many Mien people come to the Lord. I remarked quite often that God did not wait for me to do anything—it just started happening. The team I joined in Bokeo was focused on the Tai Dam people, not the Mien. When they established the company there in 1999, many Tai Dam came to the Lord and a small Tai Dam house church was planted. They met plenty of Mien people, but none of them showed any interest in the gospel. When I finished my year of language study in the capital and moved to Bokeo, however, all of a sudden Mien people started showing up at our door, literally asking to hear the gospel. I cannot claim any credit for bringing this about. It was just God's timing. The only thing I did was to ask my prayer partners in America to pray for the unreached Mien people. I think God was delighted to respond to the prayers of others for the Mien.

Another Sunday morning I was at the company by myself while my teammates were away on travels. A group of a dozen Mien people from Huay Xai showed up and asked me to tell them the gospel. I invited them in, and they sat on the floor in a circle around the front room. I began with creation and shared for more than an hour the entire biblical narrative. I explained how Jesus was God's son who died on the cross to forgive them of their sins and who rose from the dead three days later. When I was finished, they all looked at me and said, "Okay."

"Okay, what?" I asked, confused.

"Okay, we want to enter the faith. What do we do next?" I was unprepared. I had spent so much time thinking about what I would say if given the opportunity to share the gospel, I had never thought much about what to do when people accept. And I never expected they would accept it immediately. I was more prepared for rejection and rebuttal than I was for acceptance.

In any case, God worked in spite of my incompetence.

Sometimes, God works on his own, unrelated to our actions. And sometimes, he works directly through us to lead people to faith. Other times, God works in spite of our bumbling efforts, which might actually be more of a hindrance than a help. I have often felt as if God simply gave me a front row seat to see what he was doing. By the time I completed two years in Bokeo, four simple Mien churches had been planted in different villages around the province, and we helped to encourage a few more in another district that had some existing Mien Christians.

LUANG PRABANG

"How can I become a Christian? Maybe I have to pay someone to come tell me the gospel?" Tanva wondered as she sat in the Luang Prabang market, selling eggs.

The ancient royal capital of Laos and World Heritage city of Luang Prabang has a significant segment of Mien families in and around the city. This fact was one of the main reasons I decided to move there from Bokeo. There were no Mien Christians in the entire province. However, much like Bokeo, things started to happen soon after we arrived.

Along with the Hmong, many Mien people fled to Thailand during the Vietnam War and a significant number of them ended up as refugees in the United States. In both the refugee camps and the US, quite a few Mien people turned to Christ. Less than one month after we moved to Luang Prabang, one of these Mien-American Christians made a trip there to visit his relatives. He was determined to share the good news of Jesus with them. A few of the Mien elders listened but did not accept his message. They did, however, direct him to a divorced woman named Tanva.

Tanva was the daughter of a prominent Mien elder in Luang Prabang named Longva. Longva was once the tribal representative of the Mien people to Kaysone Phomvihane, the communist revolutionary leader and founder of the Lao People's Liberation Army and the second president of the Lao People's Democratic Republic. In this role, Longva traveled around Laos in a helicopter with Kaysone and also visited the Mien refugee community in the US.

During Longva's visit to the US, he was disturbed by how many Mien youth were falling into gangs, drugs, crime, and other bad behavior. He was impressed, however, by the youth of the Mien Christian community in the US. They did not appear to be following the same troubled path as the others. This noticeable difference planted a seed in Longva's mind that would bear fruit many years later.

Like many teenage Mien youth, Tanva was married at a very young age to a Mien man from a remote village in Bokeo province. When a Mien woman is married, part of the marriage ceremony is to cut ties with the ancestral spirits of her parents and join the spirits of her new husband's family. Like any other Mien bride, Tanva followed this custom. However, once in Bokeo, Tanva's new husband was not faithful to her. He often became intoxicated, beat her, and cheated on her. When it became too much, she divorced him, and took her three children with her back to Luang Prabang.

Because of her divorce, Tanva had a spiritual problem. It was impossible for her to rejoin her parents' spirits. This left her spiritually vulnerable. If she did not remarry and join another family's spirits, she would be left outside the system of spirit worship. Tanva discussed her dilemma with her father, Longva, who then suggested that she become a Christian. Tanva agreed, but didn't know what to do. She had never met a Christian before in her life.

There were at least seven chicken egg farms around the city of Luang Prabang, all owned by Mien people. The families of each of these farms sold eggs in the market, along with other products. Since Tanva's cousin owned a chicken farm, he helped set her up as an egg vendor in the market, too, so that she could make a living and raise her children. Tanva was ready to do whatever was necessary to become a Christian, but she did not know how. For six years she sat at the market selling eggs wondering how to become a follower of Jesus and save her spirit. "Maybe I have to pay someone to come tell me the gospel?" she wondered, since Mien people often hired shamans to perform spirit ceremonies when they were sick or needed a blessing. The only problem was that Tanva didn't know a Christian she could hire to solve her problem.

It just so happened that only a few weeks after we moved to Luang Prabang, a Mien man from the US, Fou Wang, visited his parents in the city. Fou Wang had come to the Lord while in the refugee camp in Thailand before moving to the US and was passionate about sharing his faith. After Longva directed Fou Wang to his daughter, Tanva accepted the Lord one Sunday morning in mid-July, 2006. We heard the news that a Mien family received Christ and met Tanva that very evening. Since Fou Wang was set to return to the US the following day, we volunteered to disciple Tanva and her daughter, Manh Meng.

Every Tuesday evening Tanva and Manh Meng came to our house. Along with my wife, Mali, we began reading together through the Gospel of Luke, verse by verse. After reading each section, we asked Tanva and Manh Meng if they understood. Invariably, they said they did not understand it. So we took time to explain the relevant meaning before progressing to the next story in the Bible. Occasionally, Tanva would have a question—usually about required ceremonies and rituals—and we would explain Christ's way of faith, grace, and love.

Over the next few months, as Tanva and Manh Meng began to understand more about the Bible, their faith grew. The Holy Spirit filled Tanva's heart with excitement and joy. She wanted to share with others. One night she broached the topic with us. "There is an older single lady at the market. She is Mien, in her 50s, and has never been married. I have told her that I am now a Christian. She is unsure if she wants to believe. Can I bring her to join us next Tuesday night?"

"Definitely!" Mali and I responded with excitement. "In fact, we would love if you can share your faith with many more Mien people. And they are all welcome to join our Bible study!" Tanva cracked a shy smile and said that she would ask this lady, Nai Fong, if she would join us, but wasn't sure if Nai Fong would be brave enough to come. We emphasized to Tanva that Nai Fong does not have to make a decision to believe in Jesus before coming and learning about him.

The next week Nai Fong joined Tanva and Manh Meng for our weekly Bible study. She had many questions. "If I believe in Jesus, and I die, what will happen to my spirit?" Death was Nai Fong's main concern. She, like the divorced Tanva, also had a spiritual problem. Without any children, she was not leaving anyone behind who could "feed" her spirit after she died. Furthermore, Mien children are responsible for performing a spirit ceremony after their parent's funeral, in order to release their parent's spirit from hell. Nai Fong was afraid that no one would do this for her and she would be stuck in hell for an eternity.

We had a great opportunity to share the good news with Nai Fong. As followers of Jesus, we are God's children. We do not "feed" him, but he takes care of us. Furthermore, Jesus rose from the dead and is alive forever—he saves us from hell, not the ceremonies performed by our descendants. He saves us from hell based upon our faith and trust in his blood, which has paid the price of our sin. Therefore, any funeral Christians perform for the deceased is for the benefit of those who are left behind—to encourage and comfort. The funeral ceremony, no matter how elaborate and expensive, does not benefit the spirit of the departed.

Our words comforted Nai Fong. By the next week she was ready to believe, and we led her to faith in Christ. All three of them were baptized at the Lao church in town led by a Khmu pastor. Nai Fong was excited!

In 2002, when I was doing Lao language study in Vientiane and discipling Kaosing, I was praying for the Mien people. It occurred to me that the Mien people did not have a Bible in their own language. I knew a Bible translation team was working on the Mien Bible in Thailand, but they were using a Roman script for the language—a script that was widely used among the Mien refugee communities in the US. However, only a few Mien people in Laos had learned English. Consequently, they had very limited familiarity with the Roman script. Accomplished Mien shamans of the highest order were familiar with Chinese characters used to express Mien, but the average Mien villager only spoke Mien—they did not read or write it. The only language they knew how to read and write was Lao, which they studied at school.

I asked Kaosing if it was possible to write the Mien language in the Lao script. He answered that it works well for some words but not so much for others, since Mien has some sounds not present in Lao. However, Kaosing and I worked out a system of combining Lao letters to represent these new sounds and developed a Lao script for the Mien language. At the same time, I connected with the lead Mien Bible translator in Thailand. Together with a computer programmer, we made it possible to transliterate Mien text instantly between Roman and Lao scripts with a stroke of a computer key. When the Mien Bible was completed and first published in 2007, it was available in Roman, Thai, and Lao scripts.

Nai Fong was not a great Lao speaker and struggled to read the Lao Bible. Embarrassed, she often deferred to Tanva and Manh Meng to read during our Bible studies. However, when I presented Nai Fong with one of the first copies of the Mien Bible in Lao script, she was able to read it very well. During the slow periods in the afternoon at the market, while all the other vendors took siesta naps, Nai Fong read and studied her Mien Bible at her own pace. It was just what she needed!

Nai Fong became a passionate follower of Christ. She was filled with joy and one Tuesday night told us that she wanted her older sister, who lived in the neighboring province of Sainyabuli, to believe in Jesus too. Mali uncharacteristically suggested that we go visit Nai Fong's sister on the weekend. All the women giggled at the thought of taking a trip together. Manh Meng pleaded with her mom to shut down their shop at the market for just one day so they could participate on this mission trip together. Tanva agreed, and our trip was set! On Saturday, we would all drive in my truck to Sainyabuli.

"How long will it take to get to her village?" I asked Nai Fong. "About two hours," was the reply. *Good*, I thought, *we would be able to go and return in the same day without having to spend the night.*

Saturday arrived and everyone loaded into my truck. This would be my first visit to Sainyabuli province. Sainyabuli was the one province in the country of Laos that was completely on the other side of the Mekong River. In 2007, there was no bridge over the Mekong between Luang Prabang and Sainyabuli provinces. Instead, trucks and cars lined up on the ramp to wait for a small ferry to take a half dozen vehicles over at a time. It had already taken almost two hours to get to the ferry, and it was clear our trip was going to take longer than we thought.

Our two-hour trip turned into five hours before we rolled into Ketpu village, deep in the heart of Sainyabuli province along a dirt and gravel road. In addition to being tired from an extra-long journey (realizing that we also had to make the 5-hour return trip in the same day), I was beginning to feel a bit leery about our presence in this remote location. We were conspicuous. We saw very few other vehicles in this remote location and no other white faces. Driving into a village with a Toyota pickup and being a foreigner, I was sure to grab people's attention. There was no way to slip in and out secretly without everyone in the village knowing we were there and asking about our purpose.

As we pulled into the village, I gave some instructions to the new believers in my truck. "We are deep in unreached territory here and as a foreigner, I stand out. We need to be careful about what we do, or someone will notify the police who could come to arrest us. Since we have to drive another five hours to get home, we do not have much time here. So, let's just talk with your sister, and if anyone asks why we are here, we will just tell them we're visiting your relatives. We can talk about life in general, and then before we leave, perhaps we can mention to her that we are Christians." Clearly, I was a bit spooked. Since we were new to Luang Prabang and Sainyabuli, I did not want to push things too far on our first visit.

I parked the truck on the side of the road, in front of Nai Fong's sister's house just as I concluded my instructions. Nai Fong's sister, Mey Fong, walked toward us, along with her twenty-something daughter, Feyta. As soon as we opened the door and before Nai Fong placed two feet on the ground, she boldly declared to Mey Fong, "You need to believe in Jesus!"

So much for my instructions.

Over the next hour, Nai Fong frantically shared her entire testimony with Mey Fong and Feyta and asked me to share the gospel. The language changed back and forth between Lao and Mien, as each of us took turns explaining the message of Jesus and what it means to follow him. The entire time we spoke, Nai Fong's niece, Feyta, listened carefully. The look on her face revealed her confusion at this strange message she was hearing for the very first time. Feyta was a "beer girl." Their family's business was to sell and serve beer. At nighttime, men from the village would come sit at their two concrete tables, drink beer, and flirt with Feyta as she served them. Feyta had one question for us, "If we become Christians can we still drink beer?"

This question, again? I thought. Right from the beginning, it seemed like alcohol would become a stumbling block and controversial issue. All of us did our best to explain God's attitude toward alcohol—that it was not categorically forbidden but that drunkenness is a sin. The nuance did not seem to satisfy Feyta, however, whose facial expression became more dumbfounded than ever. It appeared she was thinking, "Why would anyone ever believe in this strange religion?"

By the time we left, no one had decided to become a Christian. I was discouraged—not just because they did not accept the Lord, but because I could not see why unreached people like these ever would. The good news of forgiveness of sins was not such great news to them since they were not looking for redemption in the first place. They would rather find a way out of poverty and sickness. What could Jesus offer them? The trip back was much more void of excitement than the trip out had been.

At this time in Laos, many villagers were just beginning to purchase cell phones. However, in remote villages without electricity, people would charge their phones in town and then turn them off at home to save the battery. Villages like Ketpu had spotty cell phone coverage at best, so villagers would often climb to a hilltop where they could get a faint signal, turn on their phones, and call their relatives in the city. While they could call out to the city, it was next to impossible for someone in the city to call in to the village and catch them at the right moment.

More than a year after our visit, Feyta called my wife. "Mali, I have a growth on my face, and I don't know what to do!" Feyta likely wanted us to volunteer to assist her in making a trip to the city hospital to have a doctor diagnose and heal her condition. Mali suggested something else. "Let me pray for you." Over the phone, Mali prayed for Feyta's growth. Feyta thanked Mali but was probably disappointed that she did not offer more help or financial assistance.

Then it happened. In the following days, Feyta's facial growth completely cleared up! She was amazed. "Who is this God who heals us simply upon our requests, without offering him any kind of gift or animal sacrifice?" Feyta wanted to know more. She was finally convinced that our God was the real deal.

On her own, Feyta purchased passage on a truck and then a bus to travel the long distance to Luang Prabang city. She visited her aunt, Nai Fong, and then visited us. We taught Feyta from the Bible, and she was ready to place her faith in Jesus. We prayed with her to receive Christ, and the following Sunday she was baptized at the Lao church. Before returning to Sainyabuli, we gave Feyta both Lao and Mien Bibles.

"Read these every day. Pray and ask God for help. Share your faith with your family. Try to find other Christians in the area to join for fellowship." It was all we could do to encourage Feyta. Since she lived five hours away from us, it was impossible to visit her on any regular basis. Calling her was also next to impossible. There was no way to regularly disciple Feyta and follow up to see how she was doing. All we could do is pray that her faith would not be squashed by a world of disbelief around her. Feyta was an isolated sheep—a perfect target for an enemy dedicated to destroying God's work.

More than two years passed. Over this time we did not hear much from Feyta. I felt bad that we could not disciple and train her like we had with Tanva, Manh Meng, Nai Fong, and a number of others. In the fall of 2009, I attended a training in Thailand that emphasized equipping believers to share the gospel, start groups, and multiply disciples. It fit well with many ideas I had developed on my own regarding the priesthood of all believers and the challenge of working clandestinely in the context of Laos. The training gave me a vision for multiplying disciples among the Mien in Laos, and I immediately thought of Feyta. I decided we needed to bring her up to Luang Prabang for a training, along with other key Mien disciples from around the country.

"Is she even still a believer?" I wondered aloud to Mali. It was now October 2010, and we had no way to contact Feyta. "As long as she hasn't given up her faith—I want her to come to our training. Perhaps we can equip her to multiply disciples, and she will then have fellowship with others!" Mali talked with Nai Fong and asked her to send a message to Feyta. By the following week we received word that Feyta would attend our training.

Feyta was the only woman at our church multiplication training. When we began, each person introduced themselves and shared their testimony. Feyta spoke last and astounded us with what she had to say.

"In January 2007 I heard the gospel for the first time when Eliot, Mali, my aunt and others came to share with my family in Sainyabuli. Because of God's power, I became a Christian in May the following year. I was baptized here in Luang Prabang. I took the Bibles Eliot and Mali gave to me and read them at home. I didn't understand very much, but I tried to share it with others. Now I have led twelve other people in my village to believe in Jesus too!"

Twelve others! This was amazing news to us! We had feared her faith might have withered like a newly planted sapling that is never watered. Instead, Feyta flourished! I remember well the feeling I had the day we left her village. I felt like we had wasted our time and taken too great of a risk. I felt there was no way this family would ever believe, and now we might get arrested too. Certainly, God had other plans and worked in spite of my lack of faith.

Feyta loved the training and was thrilled to get some new tools for reaching out to more people. In particular, she found the Name List to be helpful. I asked each person to make a list of every non-believer they know—family members, neighbors, relatives, etc.—and pray over that list. I asked them to circle five to ten names God put on their hearts to share the gospel with next. Feyta took this to heart and returned to Ketpu village on mission.

Our next training was in February 2011, just four months later. Feyta again joined us for this training and reported that the number of believers in her village had more than doubled! The following year, in March 2012, Feyta joined us for yet another training and reported that the number grew to more than fifty. Then in May of the same year, the number of believers in Ketpu village increased to over seventy. The increase was all a result of the witness of Feyta and her disciples, who were now multiplying rapidly. In fact, it spread to the next Mien village up the road, Vanaket, where a new church was planted too. A movement had begun among the Mien of Sainyabuli province!

During this same period, we were sharing the gospel with a number of Mien families in Luang Prabang city and particularly with Kao Awn. Kao Awn was a chicken farmer, and his wife and daughters had already believed. Using chronological Bible stories, we met weekly to learn the entire Biblical narrative in an oral fashion. Kao Awn joined this group as a seeker and asked many questions. He seemed to understand but for some reason was hesitant to make a decision. One evening I visited him at his house to invite him specifically to commit to following Jesus. He acknowledged the challenge and gave indication that he would like to put his faith in Christ but needed to be ready to commit. I appreciated his desire to do it for the right reasons and not simply to placate me or his family.

The following month Kao Awn made his decision. Tears flowed down our cheeks as he walked up in front of a room packed full with Mien believers assembled for another training we were conducting and confessed his faith in Christ. Shortly thereafter, we led Kao Awn and his family, along with a few other new believers, to a beautiful garden in the mountains where each of them were baptized in a pond by Saan Lo, another Mien man we had been discipling.

Over the next few years, we conducted dozens of disciple and church multiplication trainings in Luang Prabang, hosting Mien people from every province in Laos where there were Mien communities and from every village where there were Mien churches. Some experienced persecution for sharing their faith, and a few were kicked out of their villages, leaving behind houses and land in the hands of others. But God continued to work through the simple faith of humble disciples, some of whom were disabled or had only one leg. God healed others from demon possession. Still, some struggled and fell away.

One young Mien man, Lo Ting, was tormented by evil spirits for a couple years. He was afflicted such that he could not bear to look us in the eye. He seemed to improve at times when we prayed for him only to worsen when family members continued to call in spirit priests to perform ceremonies. Lo Ting's life ended one day when the spirits told him to walk to the river and hang himself. Lo Ting's father found him dangling from a branch on the edge of the Mekong River. In spite of this, Lo Ting's mother, Meywa, put her faith in Christ.

The movement did not die, however, but continued to grow. To be sure, there are still many non-believing Mien, and many challenges ahead. Nevertheless, as Mien believers shared the gospel in each of the northern provinces, the Mien became one of the "reached" groups in the country of Laos. Many other tribes, however, had still not heard the gospel at all. One thing was becoming clear to us: wherever the gospel spread, persecution was soon to follow. Sharing the gospel in a land governed by some who wished to stamp out Christianity altogether had its perils.

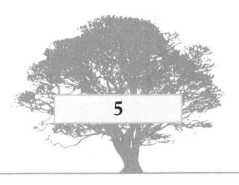

5

EARLY PERILS

GOSPEL COINS

"**B**ring his computer bag to me! I want to see all his documents." The police chief ordered his deputies to return to my truck and fetch evidence of my involvement in spreading religion. They were certain they had caught me, and it would mean permanent expulsion from the country of Laos.

I was worried, and I had good reason for it. In my computer bag were two letters from Pastor Tsoi in Bokeo. Pastor Tsoi had written to me in Lao and provided me a list of all the Mien church leaders in the province, complete with their names, villages, and phone numbers. He had also written about our work and ministry together. It would be just the evidence the communist police were looking for and the worst thing to fall into their hands.

The year was 2005 and I had just gotten married. I had spent the year in the capital, Vientiane, running paperwork and doing research for starting an agricultural company. My former colleague Austin from Bokeo visited and stayed at my house. While he was there, I cleaned out a closet and discovered a bag of aluminum coins with John 3:16 printed on them in Lao. A Mien visitor from the US had given them to me when I lived in Bokeo and I didn't know what to do with them. He had distributed a Mien language version to his Mien relatives in Laos and thought that perhaps I could use the Lao version. I threw them into a box and forgot about them.

"Do you have any use for these?" I asked Austin. He looked at them and said, "I sure do! When I drive back to Bokeo I will toss them out to the kids along the road." Austin had previously served in China and spoke Chinese fluently. When the Chinese were constructing the northern highway, he would often engage them in conversation as he traveled through and had given them some Chinese Bibles. It seemed like Austin always had a good story of how

God did something amazing when he stepped out in faith.

Austin gladly took the coins. I almost regretted that I offered them to him after I heard how he was going to use them. It sounded like fun! I planned to make multiple survey trips up to Luang Prabang before moving there, and I could have done the same thing. But I already gave them to Austin—it wouldn't be right to ask for them back.

Alas, a few weeks later, as I was rummaging through my closet, I found another bag of coins! I guess I had forgotten that the Mien visitor had given me two. *Very good.* I was set to bring them with me on my next trip north.

I waited until I hit the mountains, north of Kasi, as I ascended the paved mountain highway approaching Phou Khoun, Luang Prabang province. It was a cool and cloudy day, but no rain. I noticed a woman and her two kids walking along the road, returning home after working in the upland fields all day. They each carried woven bags, strung over their shoulders and across their bodies. The older boy had a machete in a wooden scabbard tied to his waist. The woman carried a basket with tools and items she was bringing back from the field.

I rounded the curve and just as I passed them, I tossed a handful of the aluminum gospel coins out of the window. When they hit the pavement, they produced a cacophony of clanging notes, which was like music to the children. Even though Lao currency does not make use of coins, only paper bills, it was clear they saw these as valuable. They shouted gleefully and scrambled to pick them up. I prayed they would read on the coins how God so loved the world that he gave his only son Jesus to die for them and that this would help prepare their hearts to receive the gospel when someone came to share it with them.

Handing out tracts and tossing coins was never a strategy that appealed to me. In addition to quickly flagging the authorities to your religious activities, I just did not believe it was very effective. I had always felt that the good news would be received most powerfully when it was shared in love by someone who was right in front of the listener, talking to them and ready to show them the way. I only decided to pass out these coins since Austin had given me the idea, it sounded like fun, and I thought it couldn't hurt.

It *was* fun! I tossed coins to each group of pedestrians I passed for the next three hours through the mountains of Luang Prabang province. I did not have anyone with me, and I still had to navigate the treacherous curves with one hand on the wheel and eyes on the road while making no-look coin tosses out the passenger side with the window half open. Sometimes I would miss, and a few of the coins would bounce back inside the truck, falling on the floor and between the seats. I still had almost half of the coins leftover when I arrived in Luang Prabang city.

I spent several days in Luang Prabang, and it was uneventful. I began my return trip south and prepared the leftover coins by pouring them into the console well between the front seats of the cab. I was certain I could exhaust the supply before driving out of the mountains. Tossing them out was just as enjoyable as before, as each new group of adults and kids scrambled in excitement to pick up the coins.

I paused my trip at Giugacham, the halfway point between Luang Prabang and Phou Khoun, for lunch. Giugacham was a small roadside town high in the mountain peaks. It was a common place for the buses to stop and allow their passengers to eat before continuing their journey. I parked my truck in front of my favorite roadside restaurant and enjoyed a lunch of sliced sweet pork, sticky rice, chili pepper sauce, and a cup of hot Ovaltine poured over sweetened condensed milk.

During the next leg of the trip, I threw my last coins out the window. I was glad to be done with them. I reached to pick up as many coins as I could find that had fallen to the floor. I was pretty sure I had gotten them all.

As I rolled into the district town of Phou Khoun, on the southern edge of the mountains, I noticed something strange—a bald policeman jumped up from his chair and ran parallel to the road in front of the shops and houses as I passed by. I would not have noticed him if he had not been bald, but the skin of his forehead flashing by caught my eye. I was glad to be past him, just because it was always a hassle to be pulled over by the police. Each time, they looked at your paperwork and tried to find a reason to keep your documents in order to prompt a bribe. I made it past the main three-way intersection without any issues and was confident I was in the clear. I surmised that the police officer's actions had nothing to do with me.

About five kilometers out of town, a soldier stood in the middle of the road. With his left hand he held a machine gun, and with his right hand he waved for me to stop. It was clear he was not just asking for cigarettes, as they normally do, since he was blocking the road and allowing me no option to pass. He asked for my documents, told me to turn off the truck, get out, and wait as he made a phone call. In a few minutes, a Jeep arrived with half a dozen police officers from Phou Khoun, along with the bald man I had noticed before.

The policemen descended upon my truck and began searching every nook and compartment. I asked them what they were looking for but received no reply. By this time, I knew the coins had gotten me into trouble, and I was worried they would discover one that had fallen between the seats. The police looked through my computer bag, noticed a stack of documents but did not find any coins. They whispered among themselves and then turned to me. "Come back with us to the police station in Phou Khoun!"

"Do I have a choice?" I asked. "I need to get home to Vientiane."

"You do not have a choice," they replied.

"I will go back with you if you please tell me what this is about. What are you looking for?" I demanded to know.

"We are looking for religious materials. Our chief wants to talk with you. Follow our Jeep back to the station."

I immediately thought about the letters in my computer bag from Pastor Tsoi. The police never unzipped the pocket they were in on their initial search of my bag. I thought that perhaps I could reach behind the seat into my bag as I drove the five kilometers back to Phou Khoun, feel around for the letters, pull them out and hide them somewhere else. As soon as I considered this, one of the policemen volunteered to ride with me.

The police had folded the chair of my truck forward to search the extended cab space behind the front seat. As I rolled it back into position, there on the black rubber floor mat laid one of the bright silver-colored aluminum coins. I noticed this just as the policeman was rounding the front of the truck to enter on the passenger side. I quickly snatched the coin and put it in my pocket before he opened the door to get in. Because of his presence, I could not attempt to retrieve and hide the letters in my computer bag.

The police chief was a young man. An old man would have been better. Usually, older police officers worry less about petty crimes and do not feel the need to prove their authority to others. Young officers, on the other hand, often want to display their power and demand respect. They are always the more problematic officials.

This man was no different and interrogated me for two hours. He informed me that someone saw me toss the coins out of my truck and later stop at Giugacham. There they recorded my license plate number and reported me.

He asked if I knew what was written on the coins, and I said it was a Bible verse. He asked me why I handed them out. I explained that I thought the children would like them—someone had left them with me, and I had no use for them. I told him it was common for travelers to give candy to the kids or cigarettes to soldiers along the road. "This is different!" he insisted. "This is very bad!" I was about to tell him that the coins would not rot anyone's teeth, cause diabetes, or give them lung cancer but then thought better of it.

Then he asked his deputies if they found any coins in my truck. They reported they did not. I hoped they would not search my body and find the coin in my pocket. "What did you find in the truck?" he asked them. "Just his suitcase and computer bag with documents inside," one of them replied.

"Bring his computer bag to me! I want to see all his documents," he demanded. Again, I was worried that now they would find the letters from Pastor Tsoi. This would mean certain arrest, imprisonment, and likely expulsion from the country. I had just gotten married. *What would Mali think? What would we do?* I had not yet called or texted her to tell her I was in the custody of the police.

I had the only key to my truck, so the deputies escorted me outside to open the door. My computer bag was big and heavy and wedged behind my seat in the extended cab space. As I struggled to grab the bag, I asked one of the officers, "The chief said he wanted to see the documents. Can I just bring all the documents to him instead of the entire computer bag?" They said it would be fine. So, I grabbed a stack of papers—various documents in English that had accumulated in my computer bag—and left the letters behind. *I hope this works*, I thought.

The police chief placed the stack of papers on the table in front of him. One by one, he paged through them, looking for any sign of the documents being religious in nature. A cross or picture of Jesus would seal the deal. Thankfully, nothing I had included those images. He feigned the ability to read everything printed in English, but it was obvious to me that he could not.

Occasionally he would ask me what a document was—a hotel reservation, a calendar, a list of elevations of various villages to determine appropriateness for agricultural cultivation, information about food processing, etc. At one point, he turned a page, and there before him was one of my newsletters. In bold letters across the top were the words "Mission to Laos," and they were followed by the scripture, "The people walking in darkness have seen a great light." I squirmed a little, wondering if he might decipher the meaning of this document, which caught his attention. He read the first line of the first paragraph, "May is finished. June is upon us and soon..." Then he looked up at me for a reaction, clearly wanting to impress me with his prowess of the English language. I complimented him on his ability to read English. He slightly swayed his shoulders in satisfaction, blinked slowly, and turned the page.

In the end, after a warning not to cause problems by spreading a foreign religion, they let me go. They never found any coins, and they never discovered the letters from Pastor Tsoi. There was no evidence with which to charge me. God had protected me! He also gave me valuable experience for the future in handling police interrogations.

KANPET

"I think it would be an honor to be arrested and imprisoned for the Lord."

Kanpet was not a typical Lao man and not a typical believer either. Kanpet had grown up in Vietnam. He was from the Tai Dam tribe, an animistic people who had never accepted Buddhism or Christianity. Kanpet was from a royal line within the Tai Dam people and was respected by many. But when the Vietnam War broke out, Kanpet was caught up in it. Kanpet never reported what he did or saw during the war there—it was not something he wanted to speak about—but it was serious enough to cause him to flee Vietnam and come to Laos. When the Communists took over Laos, Kanpet fled to Thailand and found himself in a refugee camp.

Like many, Kanpet heard the gospel in the Thai refugee camp. There he decided to give his life to Christ as he awaited an opportunity to emigrate to the West. An American missionary who preached the gospel to Kanpet challenged him, "Don't think for a minute that America is heaven or the promised land. You could go to America and end up being just as much a sinner as you were in Laos!" His words startled Kanpet and caused him to consider carefully what he would do.

Since many Christians had fled Laos, the missionary challenged Kanpet to return and share the gospel with the unreached people left behind. Kanpet felt God call him to take this route, and he returned to Laos. There he met a young Tai Dam woman, Manivan, and was married. Together they had two sons. In Vientiane Kanpet wanted to serve the Lord and reach his fellow Tai Dam people, but was not sure how.

Kanpet became involved with one of the LEC churches in the capital. It was there he met my colleague Austin. Austin's sending church had adopted the Tai Dam people and supported him in his efforts to reach them. Along the way, he obtained a book of the Bible in the Tai Dam language. One Sunday morning Austin had this book with him at worship services when Kanpet sat down next to him. Kanpet noticed the book and said to Austin, "That is my language!" Austin was stunned to meet a Tai Dam believer in Vientiane. They formed a friendship and partnered together to launch an effort reaching Tai Dam people in Bokeo and northern Laos.

I learned about Kanpet during my first trip to Laos in 1997. At the time, Kanpet was conducting a mission to bring relief to persecuted Htin Christians. The authorities laid siege to their village and would not allow anyone to enter or leave until they recanted their faith. Kanpet heard about their plight and organized an effort to smuggle rice to them by carrying it on their backs sack by sack through the jungle, so the Htin brothers and sisters could survive. As we traveled to Laos that summer, we prayed for Kanpet and upon arrival to Vientiane, were encouraged to learn that the mission was a success.

"Were you scared you might get caught and arrested?" Kanpet was asked. "The Lord's will be done. I think it would be an honor to be arrested and imprisoned for the Lord." Kanpet served the Lord without fear. He helped Austin start the company in Bokeo, built a house there, and started a church in the Tai Dam village where the company was located. A couple years later, Kanpet moved to Udomxai to promote agricultural production and share the gospel. He shared boldly and led people from the Khmu, Hmong, and Tai Khao tribes to the Lord. Some wondered if Kanpet's boldness would get him into trouble, but Kanpet felt his job wasn't to worry about getting arrested; it was to obey the Lord.

Shortly after Kanpet moved to Udomxai, I moved to Bokeo and rented his house. During my time in Bokeo I got to see Kanpet multiple times. I was impressed by his fearless commitment to Christ and how the Lord had used him. When I was making my own plans to start a company in Luang Prabang, I visited Kanpet and Manivan in Udomxai. Kanpet always had good insight for how to work in Laos, and I found his example helpful. It seemed that wherever he went, people made decisions to follow Christ.

We had not lived in Luang Prabang for a year when we received startling news about Kanpet. On January 18, 2007, police showed up at Kanpet's house. They handcuffed him and put him into a pickup truck. Manivan was taking a shower and barely caught a glimpse of him as the truck pulled away. Kanpet called out to her, telling her not to worry. She recognized one of the policemen and after she got herself ready, went into town to the police department along with her youngest son. However, no one at the police station admitted to her that Kanpet had been arrested. "We don't know what you're talking about," they claimed. Even the policeman she had recognized in the pickup truck said the same thing.

From that day on, Kanpet has never been heard from again. Complete silence.

The hush-hush nature of his arrest indicates that, in all likelihood, Kanpet was secretly executed. If he was alive and the police wanted a bribe for his release, which is a common practice in Laos, they would have acknowledged his arrest. But the complete silence about him meant that Kanpet's release was not an option. Manivan has suffered in anguish for years not knowing what happened to her husband. She has remained strong, however, serving the Lord and continuing to reach out to the Tai Dam.

Over the years, many have commented to me how the stories of kingdom work in Laos sound so much like the book of Acts. And while the book of Acts may appear to be a series of victories, one after another, it is also a narrative of how fierce persecution and suffering follow the expansion of the church and often propel it. Satan does not take defeat lying down—he fights for his subjects. He will use any tactic to intimidate, discourage, oppose, and even harm those who dare to pierce the darkness with the light of the good news of Jesus. It is all designed to make us stop.

In addition to promising us that we will suffer for his name, Jesus said that "forceful men" are laying hold of his kingdom. His kingdom will only be advanced by the bold and the persistent—those who are willing to suffer, even to the point of death. We should never think we are so clever that we can advance his kingdom in a way that avoids all opposition. A few years later, this opposition confronted me again.

ESCAPE FROM SAINYABULI

"We will catch them before they reach the ferry!" the police told our friends.

The news increased our anxiety, but I kept pushing down the highway. "If we can just get to Luang Prabang province, it will make it more difficult for them to do anything to us," I encouraged my family and passengers. The only problem was that the world's tenth largest river separated us from the other side, and we would have to wait for a ferry to cross! This trip was not ending as we had expected.

After seeing how God worked through Feyta to reach so many people in Ketpu village, Sainyabuli, we decided that we could equip more of them by conducting trainings in their village rather than inviting a few representatives to come to us. So in the summer of 2013, my team and I drove down to Ketpu on Friday afternoons, spent the night, and then took all of Saturday to train the believers in the new house church there. We were very nervous about doing this the first week since Ketpu was still a remote village. The road had been paved since 2007, however, and now there was much more traffic. After we finished training on Saturday, we did not linger. We departed immediately to drive all the way back to Luang Prabang, which we could do in about three hours.

On our fourth and final trip, we drove to Ketpu village on a Friday afternoon, as usual. This time, however, we brought a group of our Mien disciples from Luang Prabang to join us. The younger sister of a Mien woman we had baptized earlier that year, Chio, planned to get baptized on Sunday, the day after our training. She was from a neighboring Mien village Vanaket. Four of her family members there were also ready for baptism. Her relatives in Luang Prabang wanted to be there for the baptisms, so they accompanied us. I brought my entire family, Mali and two children, as well as our three missionary interns from the US.

Construction on the bridge over the Mekong River between Luang Prabang and Sainyabuli was underway in 2013 but was still not completed. We used the ferry to cross the river, as before. The ferry ran from about 7 a.m. until 6 p.m. After crossing over, it took about two hours to drive to Ketpu village. On previous trips, we spent the night in a small Lao town up the road from Ketpu called Nam San and never had any problems. However, people at the guesthouse were beginning to recognize us. They wondered why we kept returning to their small town.

Nam San was positioned between the two Mien villages we were visiting, Vanaket and Ketpu. Our three interns spent the night with Chio in Vanaket. The Mien believers from Luang Prabang who accompanied us stayed there too—Kao Awn, his family, and a few of his relatives. We ate dinner together in Vanaket and discussed the plans for the training on Saturday and for baptisms on Sunday.

On Saturday, we conducted our training without a hitch. We had more trainees than usual—over 30. We trained them how to prayer-walk and sent them out into the village to bless people they met. When they returned, we trained them on how to lead someone to the Lord. Finally, we learned a story about persecution from the book of Acts and discussed its implications. After prayer, we wrapped up the day in Ketpu and headed back to Nam San, where my family and I had spent the previous night.

In Nam San we ate together at the only restaurant in town, which was attached to our guesthouse. There was a group of about twelve adults, mostly Mien and three white expatriates. One of my interns at the time, Roland, was Mien-American, and he chose to spend the night in Vanaket again with the other Mien people. Our other interns chose to spend the night at the same guesthouse with us. Normally we would return home on Saturday night after concluding the training. However, we had not had any problems during the three previous weekends, and so we felt it was safe to spend a second night. Furthermore, we planned to conduct baptisms the following day. It also happened to be my daughter's fourth birthday, which we celebrated by blowing out candles on some *Eurocakes* in our guesthouse room after dinner.

At about 9 p.m. we heard a knock on our door. It was the guesthouse owner. He said a police officer was waiting outside and wanted to see Mali's passport. This was rather confusing since Mali is Lao. We were not sure if the guesthouse owner misunderstood the police, who perhaps wanted to see my passport, or if the police thought Mali was Lao-American and thus requested to see hers. Regardless, Mali boldy instructed the guesthouse owner to tell the police officer that she is Lao, that it is late and she is about to go to bed. The owner of the guesthouse obliged and left our room. I was certain he would immediately return with the police officer demanding us to come outside, but we watched through the window as the police officer left.

His departure did not comfort me. I knew that in the morning they would certainly detain and question us. If that were to happen, they would likely hold us for a day or more and interrogate us about our purpose and activities. I also knew that it would probably conclude with a report and warning about not interacting with local believers. Nevertheless, I did not want to go through the stress of an interrogation with our children in tow. I considered returning to Luang Prabang immediately. However, the only problem was that it was too late to cross the Mekong River. It had already been three hours since they shut the ferry down for the night, and it was a two-hour drive away.

I spent the next two hours talking to our interns and the Mien brothers and sisters on the phone. We learned that the village headman of Vanaket had called one of the local believers to come see him that morning. This was not a coincidence. We were certain he had asked this believer about our activities. The most likely scenario was that the village headmen subsequently reported us to the Nam San police.

I decided that the best thing to do was to leave early in the morning so we could get to the ferry right when it opened at 7 am. Our plan was to be on the first trip across the river and out of Sainyabuli province before any of the police would start work for the day. So, I settled the bill with the guesthouse, while Mali and the kids fell asleep. Then, I removed all the lesson materials from my bags and burned them one by one in the bathroom. I flushed the ashes down the toilet.

We got up at 4:30 and quietly packed all our bags into my truck. We lifted our sleeping kids out of bed, and the interns helped to situate them inside the cab. We pulled out of the guesthouse at 5 a.m. It was still dark, and most everyone was still asleep. However, it turned out that the police station was adjacent to our guesthouse. A man standing in front of the station watched us drive away.

We made good time on the highway and arrived in Sainyabuli city at around 6 a.m. If the police officer had alerted authorities there, it would be a likely place for a roadblock. Thankfully, we encountered none. Then, just as we made it through town, we received a call from our other intern Roland.

Roland whispered as he spoke. "The police are here. I heard them say, 'We will catch them before they cross the ferry!'" He was sleeping on the upper level of the house, and the police were down below interrogating our Mien friends about us and about their own Christian activity. We became nervous again but prayed for Roland and our friends as we drove.

We passed numerous police boxes along the way but there was no sign of activity in any of them. No police came out to pull us over or even watch as we drove by. We did not see any police officers, in fact, until we arrived at the boat ferry around 6:45 a.m. Luang Prabang province was waiting on the other side of the Mekong River.

As we approached the ramp to wait for the ferry, we noticed a policeman sitting on a motorcycle. He looked at our truck and then followed us down the boat ramp, parking where we had stopped. Our anxiety spiked. *Oh, they got us!* I thought. We all sat quietly trying our best not to look nervous. The policeman took a few steps toward our truck, looked past us, and shouted something to a lady down the ramp. Then he mounted his bike and drove off. *Whew!* He was not looking for us.

We continued to wait for the ferry to start transporting vehicles. Because of the number of cars ahead of us, we did not make it on the ferry until the second trip across. We arrived on the Luang Prabang side a little after 7 a.m. We felt a little relieved at this point, but were still worried about Roland and our Mien friends. After a quick call, we learned that the police had left them. We were concerned, however, that the police might still track us down, so we proceeded directly to Luang Prabang without stopping for breakfast.

We arrived home safely. There were no more issues on the last leg of our journey. The police told our Mien friends that they were suspicious of us for having left so early. However, we were not under any orders to stay, and early travel is common in Laos. Unfortunately, the Mien believers gave the police our names, our village of residence in Luang Prabang city, and told them about our business. But thankfully, there were no further repercussions.

The narrow escape did not shake the faith of the Mien believers either. In fact, as soon as the police officers departed, they turned to one another and said, "Let's worship and baptize these new believers!" They conducted a simple worship service in their home led by Kao Awn, who we had discipled over the course of the previous year. Afterward, making use of the large concrete water basin in their washroom, Kao Awn baptized all five of the new believers into Christ.

A CLOSE CALL

Over the years, I developed a knack for smuggling. Of course, I never smuggled narcotics, weapons, or people. But I did smuggle Bibles and other Christian materials. There was no other way to bring these things to people inside of Laos. Laos does not have freedom of the press. One must submit any official printed material to the Ministry of Information and Culture, await a long process, and then be approved or rejected for sale and distribution in the country.

I was familiar with this process. I had once published a language book and obtained approval. However, the chances of getting Christian material approved were nil to none—especially not materials that taught how to "multiply Christian disciples and churches" throughout the entire country. Consequently, we often brought in only a few boxes of Bible stories, radios, CDs, or training manuals at a time.

On one trip home, I felt particularly bold and brought more than 10 boxes of chronological Bible stories across the border. My family was with me, and we hid the boxes under a tarp. We arranged food, home supplies, and suitcases on top of the boxes and then under another layer of tarp. We understood exactly where the police would pull up the tarp to inspect, and we knew they did not want to go through the hassle of unloading everything. But there was always the chance they could.

On this occasion, the immigration officials had stamped all our passports and vehicle paperwork. We returned to our truck and drove up to the gate. A police officer at the gate would typically inspect our documents to make sure they were stamped, glance in the bed of the truck, and then wave us through. Occasionally they would pull up the tarp to peek or ask us what we were hauling. This time, a group of four officers stopped us. The head officer looked in our window and asked us questions, while one of the younger ones became curious about what the tarp was hiding. He pulled it up to peer inside and was poking around as if he wanted to dig deeper.

Being a mixed family, Lao and American, we are a curiosity to most Lao people. Typically, they love the look of mixed children and the head officer asked us about our kids. We answered all his irrelevant personal questions and mentioned that our kids go to a Lao-English international school in the city. Then, to the delight of everyone, and quite unprompted, my little daughter started singing the Lao national anthem. The head officer smiled and beckoned the others to come see this cute American-Lao girl sing the nation's most patriotic song. The young officer was still interested in the contents of our truck, but the head officer ignored him, waving him to come see her sing. When she finished the song, he handed us our paperwork, and promptly waved us through.

On another occasion, I may have gotten too bold.

I was returning to Laos from Chiang Mai, Thailand, where I had retrieved the largest print run we had ever done of our evangelism and church planting training manuals in the Lao language. A partner in the US helped to fund a printing of 650 training and leaders' manuals. I picked them up in Chiang Mai, along with some business brochures we printed for our company. Altogether, I had 22 boxes in my truck, 17 of which were the Lao training manuals. One of the boxes of business brochures was not taped shut because it was only half-full.

I packed these boxes into my truck and hid them under groceries and suitcases, again relying upon my experience. It was rare that I returned to Laos without something I needed to hide in my truck. I had a 1.000 batting average in getting things in, even when being inspected. But on this steamy autumn evening, things got a little dicey.

I exited Thailand without a hitch and headed over to the Lao side. Both Immigration and Customs stamped all my paperwork, but as I drove through the Customs inspector stopped me. They had checked like this many times before. It was standard practice. I had always been able to get through or talk my way through, if necessary. On this night, however, the Customs inspectors were checking all of the vehicles very closely.

They looked into the heart of the extended cab space in my truck and dug under several items until they found some of the boxes I was transporting. One of the officials snapped a picture. *That was new!* I had never seen photos taken before, and it concerned me.

"What is in these boxes?" the older one demanded. "Open one up right now and show me!" My heart started pumping rapidly and sweat poured from my forehead. I did not see a way out of the situation! I could only imagine what would happen when they read the Lao title of our training manuals.

"Wait, I have a box that is already open!" I thought quickly. "Let me show you the contents from that box." I hastily untied the ropes on the bed of my truck, pulled back the tarp and grabbed the open box of business brochures. The boxes in the cab, which the officials had discovered, were training manuals, not brochures. Amazingly, they never considered that the boxes might each contain different materials. After I produced a pack of brochures, they assumed they were all the same. The officials never questioned if there was anything else inside the boxes.

For a moment, I thought I had successfully used a Jedi mind trick: *These aren't the manuals you're looking for.* But it did not get me through.

The Customs inspectors looked at the business brochure and then ordered me to unload all the boxes. I tried to delay them, "I'm happy to do all the official paperwork and pay any taxes for the brochures." I had undergone this process before with equipment and supplies.

"Do you have the receipt?" they asked. "I do!" I replied with a bit of hope. I dug the receipt out of my computer bag and handed it to them. "Give us your passport," they requested. This was not unusual, so I handed it to them too, even though the customs booth had already stamped me in. They held on to my passport the entire time. "Pull ahead and park your truck over there as we prepare the paperwork." I parked past the gate as they drew up the documents to take to their boss.

The boss wasn't having it. He looked at an example of the brochure and said it must be approved by the Ministry of Information and Culture. He refused to let me in with the boxes. "Unload all your boxes here and we will keep them in our quarantine room. Then, you can obtain approval and return on Monday with the proper paperwork to retrieve them." It was Saturday night. Waiting until Monday would mean that the boxes would be in their custody for thirty-six hours or more.

Leaving the boxes with Customs was not a viable option. If I did, they would certainly inspect them much more closely and discover that they were not all business brochures but Christian training materials. In some ways, discovering these manuals would be worse than even Bibles. Bibles, they could presume, are for those who are already Christians. But the title of these manuals declared in Lao: Reproducing Christian Churches in an Abundant Multiplying Way. They represented the very thing anti-Christian elements in the communist party feared the most. If discovered, the police would place me under arrest and destroy the manuals. I wanted to do anything to keep from unloading the boxes. At this point, however, I was afraid I did not have a choice.

I pleaded with the boss, kneeling next to his desk. I begged him to allow me to pay all appropriate taxes. "There is no other way but leaving all of the boxes in our custody," he insisted. "It doesn't matter how much you pay, I will not let them through!" I waited for almost an hour, hoping that a delay tactic might move him, but the boss would not budge. Time was on his side. In a few minutes, the border would close, and I would be stuck. I asked him what we could do to get through. Clearly annoyed by my pleas, he finally snapped at me, "If you don't want to turn the boxes over to us then you'll have to take them back to Thailand!"

When he said this, I saw a possible way out of the situation without getting arrested or losing the materials. "Okay, I'll go back to Thailand," I said to his astonishment, "and do the paperwork later." The other Customs officials were confused, but they allowed me to drive around to the other side of the facility to check back out of Laos.

The entire time, several police officers witnessed my interactions with Customs, looked at my passport, but never inspected my truck.

One of the customs officials escorted me to the other side and explained to the Immigration and Customs officials there why I was leaving. The police on the exit side of the facility did not inspect my truck either. It should have been a huge red flag to them—someone has something in their vehicle that they do not want officials to see. It could have been drugs, weapons, or other contraband they might typically expect. But they seemed to be convinced it was nothing more than the business brochures I had produced and that I was only trying to avoid the hassle. God was taking care of me.

I left all the materials with a friend in the Thai border town of Nong Khai and holed up in a guesthouse for the night. The next morning I passed through the border without any issues, minus the brochures and manuals.

A few weeks later, Mali was able to get all 22 boxes across the border in two trips. One of her relatives is an important government official from a southern province in Laos. He happened to be visiting Vientiane and allowed Mali to use his truck to cross over to Thailand. Because his truck has the blue government plates, Customs never inspects them. Mali was able to drive right past them without any issues.

In Isaiah 43:1-3 (NIV), God said to his children, "Do not fear, for I have redeemed you; I have summoned you by name; you are mine. When you pass through the waters, I will be with you; and when you pass through the rivers, they will not sweep over you. When you walk through the fire, you will not be burned; the flames will not set you ablaze. For I am the LORD your God, the Holy One of Israel, your Savior."

My experiences have shown me that this promise is true. God does not promise to prevent our exposure to waters. He does not promise to keep us from rivers and fire. In fact, he will lead us into all of them. The more we follow in the footsteps of Jesus, the more rivers and fires we will face. His promise, however, is that he will bring us through. I have experienced the exhilaration and joy on the other side of trials, when you have miraculously survived. But I also found that arriving safe on the opposite bank did not increase the appeal of crossing. I was just as prone to avoid danger as I was before.

God is never finished with us. As long as we have breath, we cannot just coast. We cannot point to past trials and victories and claim that our ticket has been punched. He continues to lead us on. There are more fires he will lead us through, and more miraculous victories to experience. God never allows us to get to a point where we can cease having faith in him.

I remember first talking with my friend and partner, Nick. Each of us had led major projects in Laos. Both of us had affected a particular unreached people. Yet, God had a greater vision. We were not done; we were only getting started. Did we have the stomach for it? It would most certainly mean a lot of work and more trials. There is no giving birth without the pains of labor.

We felt that God was saying to us, "It is too small a thing for you to be my servant [to reach the Mien.]… I will also make you a light for [all the tribes in Laos], that my salvation may reach to the ends of the earth."

God loves to open our eyes beyond what we could ask or imagine. We must trust him and press on as long as we have breath. God showed us that planting a church among an unreached people group was a wonderful blessing, but seeing them multiply to many generations and tribes was even better. Going forward, one common phrase in the Bible began to have much more meaning to me: Be fruitful and *multiply*.

MULTIPLY

THE GAP

"**H**ow many people are in the tribe you're praying for?" The training facilitator asked a volunteer to write the population of their adopted unreached people group on the whiteboard. After some clarification from others about national boundaries and diaspora groups, he wrote down a number.

1,400,000.

"Now, how many of them will hear the gospel for the first time in a given year?" He gazed at the room of young missionaries with a serious look on his face. "Not those who have already heard it and will hear it again for a second or third time this year, but how many will hear the message of Christ for the *first* time in the next year?"

Of course, no one knew the answer. The facilitator told us to give him our best guess. "Maybe 100?" someone ventured. The group in question did not have but more than a handful of Christians and no one from the outside was sharing the gospel with them as far as anyone knew. No Christian radio broadcast existed in their language, and only a small percentage could speak the national dialect.

"Okay, but let's assume there are Christians out there sharing the gospel with this group, and we just don't know about them," the facilitator continued. "In fact, let's be generous. Let's assume we've grossly underestimated the level of evangelism among these people. Let's say, for example, that 1,000 people hear the gospel for the first time each year."

The entire room chuckled. We were not sure if the reality was ninety, one hundred or two hundred people, but we were confident that nowhere near one thousand people were hearing the good news message of Christ for the first time, each year, every year! There were just not that many efforts being made for this number to be true. But the facilitator asked us to humor him.

He glared seriously at the participants once more. "Now, assuming this is true... how long before they all hear about Jesus?" It was not a rhetorical question. He wanted us to do the math and give an answer.

"Let's see... 1.4 million people divided by 1,000 people per year.... That means we'll accomplish the task in... 1,400 years!" *Whoa! That's a long time.* Sobering, actually.

The group assumed his point was that we need to get busy and get going. It was not.

The facilitator asked us to consider how many of those 1.4 million people will be here 1,400 years from now. The answer: None. Where did they go? They're all dead. Their children are dead. Their great grandchildren are dead. Their great-great-grandchildren are all dead! In fact, after 1,400 years, more than forty generations of this people group will have been born, lived their lives, and died. At this rate, the gospel will *never* reach this entire people group!

"That's not cuttin' it, folks!" the facilitator exclaimed. "In fact, even if we increased the number of people hearing the gospel for the first time to ten thousand people per year, that still means it would take 140 years to reach them all if their population never turned over." However, in 140 years, more than three generations would have come and gone, and it is still not fast enough. *How can we possibly ever reach them all?*

There is a huge gap between the rate of population change and the rate at which we are sharing the gospel. Short of some form of mass media, how can we share the message of Christ more than ten thousand times per year?

MANGO TREES

"What is the fruit of a mango tree?" It was my turn to be the facilitator. I asked one of the participants to draw a picture of a mango tree on the board.

"A mango!" they answered easily.

"Very good!" I said and asked the volunteer to draw mangos on the mango tree. "It doesn't grow watermelons or pineapples, right?" The young Lao, Khmu, and Mien men and women laughed.

"For what purpose does the mango tree produce mangos?" I continued my inquiry. The answer was too obvious to the group. "So, we can eat them!" one of the talkative young men answered as everyone started licking their lips thinking about freshly picked ripe mangos. "No, it's so we can sell them at the market!" another one countered. More chuckled and admitted that he was right. One way or another, we will fill our bellies or our wallets with the produce of the mango tree!

"So, if the mango tree is the mother, and the mangos are her children..." I paused for effect, "...she has children so that we can eat them?" The room erupted in laughter. No one has children so that another species can eat them. So, I asked them again, "From the perspective of the mango tree—why does it produce mangos?"

They caught on quickly. Inside the mango is a seed. If the seed falls to the ground, is fertilized by the rotting mango fruit, and left undisturbed, it will grow into another mango tree! In fact, from the perspective of the mango tree (and any living organism that reproduces), the purpose of offspring is to continue the survival of the species—to spread and multiply its kind. Consequently, the real fruit of a mango tree is not just a mango, but another mango tree. Because mango trees do not produce only one mango, but many, the real fruit is *many* more mango trees.

How about for the follower of Christ? I urged them to wield "ears to hear" the deeper meaning and application of this illustration.

MR. BIG AND MR. LITTLE

Mr. Big was a talented evangelist. When he spoke, people's eyes were opened. The Spirit moved. They turned to Christ in droves. In fact, Mr. Big was such a powerful speaker that he led ten thousand people to Christ each year.

Mr. Little was not so talented. He did not know how to speak in front of huge crowds. He did not know all the answers from the Bible. He was not particularly charismatic or attractive. Though he loved the Lord just like Mr. Big, he was only able to lead three people to Christ in one year.

Which would you rather have—three or ten thousand?

Here's the thing about Mr. Big and Mr. Little—Mr. Big was so busy leading throngs of people to Christ, he had to keep moving on and finding more people to hear him preach. Getting ten thousand people to make decisions for Christ each year meant that he had to baptize almost two hundred people per week. He did not have a lot of time to teach, train, or encourage them. After leading them to the Lord and baptizing them, he would continue on to the next batch.

Mr. Little had more time. He decided that he would use the entire year to teach, train and equip his three new disciples in how to know and serve the Lord. In fact, he decided he would show them how to make disciples of their own, whom they could then encourage and train and continue the same process. So that is what he did. And though he didn't reach nearly as many people as Mr. Big did in a year, Mr. Little's process worked, and his disciples soon had disciples of their own.

After one year, Mr. Big had baptized ten thousand new converts. Mr. Little had his three, plus himself, for a total of four.

After the second year, Mr. Big won another 10,000 people to Christ, and combined with his fruit from the previous year, his total number of disciples doubled to 20,000. Mr. Little and his disciples each made 3 more disciples in the following year, which represented 12 new believers. Combined with the original 4, his group grew to 16 disciples—a multiple of 4! Still, Mr. Little's group size was miniscule compared to the large impact of Mr. Big.

In the third year, the two processes continued to bear fruit in the same manner as before. Mr. Big added another 10,000 to his number for a total of 30,000, and Mr. Little's group each won 3 more people to Christ and their total number multiplied by 4 to 64.

This continued in the same way for the next three years. Mr. Big's believers grew from 30,000 to 40,000 to 50,000 to 60,000. Mr. Little's group went from 64 to 256 to 1,024 to 4,096—all because each year, each one of them won 3 more people to Christ and discipled them to win 3 more the following year and to repeat the process. But it just didn't seem like they were having as much of an impact as Mr. Big. Reaching 4,000 disciples was a great number but still dwarfed by Mr. Big's 60,000—more than 10 times as many! Mr. Big was starting to become quite popular and was often asked to speak at large conferences. Mr. Little, on the other hand, never had a crowd of more than twenty to thirty people. He had encouraged his disciples to train people to meet in their own homes, so as a result, none of their groups grew very large.

Mr. Big continued at his break-neck speed of winning 10,000 more people to Christ every year. In years seven, eight, and nine his total number grew to 70,000 then 80,000 and then 90,000 converts. Mr. Little and all of his six generations of disciples continued each to win 3 more people to the Lord every year and to train them to repeat the process. They did so faithfully, and their total number, now scattered across the city in many small groups, grew from 4,096 to 16,384 in year seven to 65,536 in year eight and finally 262,144 people in year nine!

Whoa! Do you see what just happened? In year nine, Mr. Little's total number of disciples grew to more than double that of Mr. Big's! Just three years before he had less than one-tenth of Mr. Big's number. After nine years of faithful ministry, and over 90,000 converts to show for it, Mr. Big was starting to get tired. It was a lot of work. Mr. Little and his disciple-makers and trainers, however, were just getting started.

What would happen next? Let's see!

Mr. Big recommitted to his faithful ministry, and over the next eight years, he continued to get the exact same incredible results by winning 10,000 more people to Christ every single year:

Year 10:   100,000
Year 11:   110,000
Year 12:   120,000
Year 13:   130,000
Year 14:   140,000
Year 15:   150,000
Year 16:   160,000
Year 17:   170,000

In the same time period, the disciple multiplication movement started by Mr. Little was just beginning to gain momentum. After being led to faith in Christ, each of them were discipled, equipped, and trained to lead 3 more people to Christ each year and to disciple, equip, and train them, too, to repeat the process. These were the results as their total number increased by a factor of 4 each year:

Year 10:   1,048,576   (moved beyond their city)
Year 11:   4,194,304
Year 12:   16,777,216   (moved beyond their state)
Year 13:   67,108,864
Year 14:   268,435,456   (nearly saturated the USA)
Year 15:   1,073,741,824   (saturated the western hemisphere)
Year 16:   4,294,967,296   (now also Africa and Europe)
Year 17:   17,179,869,184 (ran out of people on earth!)

Seventeen years. In less than seventeen years, Mr. Little's approach of each person making three new disciples each year and equipping them to repeat the process won every single person on earth.

Mr. Big was still in his hometown.

After sharing the story of Mr. Big and Mr. Little with those attending our training about how to multiply disciples and churches, I asked the participants to share insights they discovered from this parable.

"Which approach produces stronger and more mature believers?" I asked. It did not take long for them to reply. "Mr. Big never asked them to do anything! All they did was sit, listen, and receive Christ. But with Mr. Little, new believers were immediately put to work making more disciples!"

"How about persecution?" I continued to probe for lessons learned, "Which approach is more immune?" The training participants sat silent mulling the question. Finally, one of them spoke up. "Well, if I was a policeman and I saw the thousands of people Mr. Big was winning to Christ, all I would have to do is arrest or kill him. Then it would all stop. But if I arrested Mr. Little, it wouldn't stop anything—his disciples would keep on going!"

He hit the nail on the head. One approach was dependent upon a singular charismatic persona, Mr. Big, who became quite famous in his movement because he was the one who led each person to Christ. In the other approach, Mr. Little's, only Jesus became famous. It multiplied because it did not depend upon one man to do all the work.

Many Lao pastors are doing their best to become like Mr. Big. They have settled into ministry models not conducive to multiplication. It was my hope that we could prevent our disciples from falling into the same ruts and take an approach more like Mr. Little's.

When the President of the Lao Evangelical Church received a copy of our training manual and studied the example of Mr. Big and Mr. Little, the message inspired him. He decided to include the lesson in his authorized "Multiplying Disciples and Churches" training. He and official LEC trainers have now taught this curriculum to thousands of Lao believers throughout the country.

In our training, however, some of the more experienced participants realized that the parable's example was too perfect. "No one wins ten thousand people to Christ each year for seventeen years, and not every disciple we make will faithfully repeat the process and win three more people to Christ each year for seventeen years!"

They were correct. I explained that as a parable, the examples were ideal and meant only to illustrate a couple points.

The first is that we will have the greatest potential for impact when we get out of the way, train up others to take our job, and not insert ourselves into positions of importance and fame. If we make ourselves too important, too popular, too much in control, we may produce some immediate results that are quite impressive. But we will also become the poison pill to the potential of a movement that goes well beyond our personal reach.

The second lesson is that we will never reach the masses if our approach does not multiply. The math just doesn't work. Any approach that increases by addition will never make headway unless our target group is extremely small. But with even a little multiplication, an entire population segment can be reached within a single generation.

MISSIONS AND MULTIPLICATION

If we understand the Bible in terms of God's mission, we can better interpret much of what it says. It will also help us to understand what missions actually is and why multiplication is critical.

My experience in missions has been a long journey. In my early days, anything done in another country or language was considered missions if it came with a Christian label. Formal studies in missiology, extensive reading about missiological issues, multiple internships on different fields, and well over a decade of language learning and business and church planting experience in Laos have helped to mold my perspective. Beyond all of this, however, a deeper understanding of the Word of God and its message have altered and formed my views significantly.

Missions is defined by Christ, not by us. We can never understand what our mission is—what the church's mission is—if we do not understand what God's mission is. We may try to broaden the definition or adjust it to what we assume is holistic from a human perspective, but I have found it helpful to focus upon God's primary and ultimate purpose for sending Jesus to earth. For what reason did Jesus come?

For so long I had it wrong. I assumed Jesus came to establish his church, or found Christianity (to "make the world a better place"). Christianity was an institution that filled the religious aspect to human society. When faith is relegated to a sector in one's life rather than its core, it's easy to take an institutional view of the church. According to this view, the religious institution of church, or Christianity, exists in our lives to perform critical ministerial and charitable functions as needed.

I do not see it this way any longer. Instead of an institutional view of Church, I now hold a *missional* view of Church. That is, the church does not exist to perform religious ceremonies in perpetual service to a static society. However, the church exists to accomplish a task or mission that God has entrusted to us in a dynamic world that is approaching a conclusion.

God's plan is not to create a utopia on earth. His plan is to replace it. God's utopia is heaven. The Bible is quite clear that there is a coming judgment. Before that time, society will grow increasingly wicked and the earth will be destroyed. In its place, he will create a new heaven and a new earth. This does not mean we should trash the earth we are living in or shirk our responsibility as stewards of God's creation. But it does mean that we are living in the middle of a short window in eternity—the time between the first and second comings of Christ. We live *after* his first coming, in which he lived, taught us, died, and rose again to bring forgiveness and reconciliation to all who trust in him. But we live *before* his second coming, in which he will return with power to judge the nations. All people will stand before his throne. A great sorting will occur at judgment, to which many parables of Jesus attest, when sheep are separated from goats, good fish from bad fish, wheat from weeds, and grain from chaff. One will survive; the other will perish.

In this interval, we have much work to do that will greatly affect this sorting. In the interim, we have his mission. It is his mission, not ours, but he has commissioned us to fulfill his purpose on earth.

I love the words of 2 Peter 3:9 (NIV) in which Peter says, "The Lord is not slow in keeping his promise as some understand slowness. Instead he his patient with you, not wanting anyone to perish, but everyone to come to repentance."

What was the slowness to which Peter was referring? It was Christ's return— his second coming. Peter and others were eyewitnesses of Jesus's ascension to heaven when he promised that he would return. Jesus commissioned his followers to make disciples of all nations, and told them that the gospel of the kingdom would be preached as a testimony to all nations, and then the end would come. But when Peter wrote these words to encourage Christians, it had been thirty or so years since Christ had ascended to heaven. They had expected Jesus to come back already. *Where was he? Why was he taking so long?* Even worse, some of the older believers had died. *How does that work? I thought we would live forever!* It was a confusing time for the Christian community.

Peter explains that Christ's delay in returning wasn't because he was slow to get around to it but that he was patiently waiting for more people to repent so that they could be saved from eternal destruction. After he returns, there will be no more opportunity to switch sides. Clearly, before Jesus returns to judge the earth, he wants all peoples to have the opportunity to hear and respond to the gospel. That is the mission he has given to us, which completes his mission of redemption and reconciliation of mankind to God.

How can we complete this mission? At the rate we're going, we are barely keeping up. It will take an approach that multiplies to narrow the gap between those who have the gospel and those who have yet to hear. How can we make headway? How can we give everyone on earth the opportunity to hear and respond to the good news of Jesus?

First, we must understand that it will take multiplication. Second, we must realize that we are engaging in a spiritual war. There are forces opposed to multiplication and the spread of faith.

SATAN'S THREE STRATEGIES

The word "mission" is also a military term. Soldiers and armies fighting in a war, attempting to accomplish their mission, have an enemy who opposes them. The same is true for the spiritual battle we are fighting in our quest to accomplish the mission God has given us. We have an enemy, and he does not want us to succeed!

In Matthew 13 Jesus tells the parable of the sower who appears to cast seeds randomly on four different types of land—a hardened path, rocky ground, thorny turf, and good soil. Each of the first three have their problems, but the fourth is the prime example. The work of the gospel progresses a bit further with each type of soil.

In the first, the path, the seeds never even germinate. They stay on top of the packed surface, and the birds quickly snatch them away. In the second, the seeds penetrate the shallow soil and sprout up readily. However, because of the rocks, their roots do not develop, and they wither and die when the sun appears and scorches them. In the third soil, the seeds fall among the thorns, and the plants grow right up, as they did in the second soil. Now, if you pay close attention to the text, you will notice that these plants do not die—they remain alive! The thorns do not kill the plants; they only make them unfruitful. Finally, in the fourth soil, the seeds grow and produce a crop up to one hundred times what was sown.

Jesus tells us that the seed is the message of his kingdom—the gospel. If we understand the germination to be the acceptance of this message and the new life in Christ we find, we can best understand the meaning of the entire parable. In the first soil, the message is not accepted at all—it is rejected outright. People never become Christians. In the second soil, the message is accepted but then later renounced because of persecution and hardship. People become Christians and then later recant, leaving the faith. In the third soil, the message is never repudiated. People remain believers, but they are never fruitful. The busyness of life and concern for wealth makes them unfruitful in their faith. But in the fourth soil, not only are the people fruitful in their faith, they multiply many times over.

Do we have ears to hear the meaning of this parable? If the seed sown is the message of the kingdom—the gospel—then what is the fruit that is born by the fourth soil? Is it not the same as the seed that is sown? And if that is the case, is not the fruitfulness the re-sharing of the gospel with others? Is not the fruitfulness the multiplication of faith to many more people? This parable is about multiplication. And it is clear that this is what Jesus wants.

If we understand the mission of Jesus on earth, we also see in this parable Satan's strategy to thwart God's mission. Satan does not want to see God succeed in his mission. He does not want to see more people redeemed out of the prison of sin in which he has them locked. He opposes God's purpose and mission—it is his primary aim until the end. As such, we can see his strategies in this parable.

STRATEGY 1: OUTRIGHT REJECTION

The seed never even penetrated the hardened soil of the path. It never had a chance to germinate. Instead, it was quickly snatched away. This happens anytime someone immediately rejects the message of God, for any reason, without taking time to consider its truthfulness. It could be that they hear and *don't* understand (as if it were spoken in another language) or that they hear and *refuse* to understand. In any case, they do not give the message a chance.

It has been said that most people who reject Christianity do so not because they find it to be false, but because they perceive it to be foreign. *It's not for me. It doesn't belong to me—it belongs to you.* Many feel Christian faith is for those who are old and about to die, for those who are already "good" people, or for those who belong to a particular subculture or political party. It is seen as "other," so it is rejected before it is ever truly considered. *I have no interest in becoming what you are* (culture, race, politics, etc.) *or joining your community, so I do not want to become a Christian.*

It is a favorite strategy of Satan, and one of his most effective. How better to combat the saving power of the gospel than to never give it any oxygen?

But what if it doesn't work? What if Satan's strategy of getting people to reject the gospel outright fails and some people listen and decide to follow Jesus? In this case, Satan turns to his Plan B.

STRATEGY 2: TURN UP THE HEAT

When the seed germinates and grows, it begins fresh and vigorous. Like many new believers whose faith is young, it is exciting and full of joy. The honeymoon of forgiveness is thrilling. But now Satan must act quickly to employ his second strategy, designed specifically to get them to give up what they've already accepted. He must do this while they are young, new, and excited and have shallow roots. So, he turns up the heat on them.

Persecution, opposition, and difficulties fall upon the new believer. Any trial can be spun by Satan to discourage young Christians. Before they get too committed, he wants to give them the feeling that they've made a mistake, been deceived, or that faith just doesn't work in the real world.

Unfortunately, many turn away. Especially those who are won to Christ with a message of prosperity and the hope that all of life's problems will just fade away. Instead, it seems like hardships abound, and it's no longer worth the trouble to continue following Christ. The scorching sun of adversity and persecution causes those with no root in the Word to wither and die.

But what if this strategy also fails? What if some of the new believers do not turn away? What if they do root themselves in Christ and persist in their faith? Then Satan turns to his next strategy.

STRATEGY 3: CONTAIN

With these believers, Satan failed to get them to reject the gospel outright and he failed to get them to renounce their faith in Christ. Whatever Satan tried he could not win these people back into his kingdom. His only option now is to contain—to make sure their faith in Christ doesn't spread to anyone else! How does he accomplish this? By filling their lives with so many distractions that they do not have any margin for spreading their faith to others. These are the thorns.

For a long time, I misread this parable. I assumed the thorns choked out the plants until they died. But the scriptures never say that the plants died because of the thorns. It says that the thorns choked the plants. A better word might be "smothered" with the image of the plants being crowded out by too many weeds. Consequently, the thorns made them *unfruitful*. Only the fruit of the plant gives a harvest, and only from the harvest can the seed for next year's crop come.

I have been a Soil #3 Christian for much of my life—too busy or distracted by so many good things or worldly pursuits to re-plant my faith in the lives of others. Many of us in the church are right here—we have succumbed to Satan's third strategy. He knows it is unlikely that we will ever renounce our faith, deny Christ, or turn away from the church. So, he takes our focus off Jesus's mission and *contains* our faith.

Our faith is contained when we relegate it to be only an occasional part of our life, such as when we attend church services or Christian events. Instead, our lives become focused more upon our families and careers, and other pursuits command our attention. As a result, faith never expresses itself outside these intermittent recreations. Additionally, our faith is contained when we get involved in church activities that keep us around other Christians 100% of the time. We become buried deep within the Christian community and never have any contact with those outside of Christ.

If Satan does not get us at Strategy 1 or at Strategy 2, he gets most of us here. Satan has been doing an excellent job at containing the Christian faith for centuries, with some notable exceptions. He is not satisfied losing any of his subjects over to God, but he can survive as long as faith does not spread. His kingdom will persist as long as Christians do not multiply.

What does it take to be the exception? What does it take to live on mission with God and remain completely focused upon redeeming people in this world to him? How much faith will we need to multiply 30, 60, or 100 times over? This is the challenge Jesus presents to us in his parable. We must remove hardness, rocks, and weeds from our lives. Only the good soil produces multiplication, and as a result, only the good soil accomplishes his mission.

I'll let you in on a secret. Satan has yet another strategy. And this one may be his absolute favorite. It comes before Strategy 1. In fact, we might call it Strategy 0. This is Satan's most effective strategy of all: Keep the soil from ever having any seed tossed upon it. Do not allow people ever to hear the good news message of Jesus at all. Strategy 0 is zero sharing of the good news. People cannot accept a message they never hear.

We often do not know what kind of soil our seed is falling upon when we share God's message with people. Will they reject it outright? Will they accept it and later turn away? Will they persist in faith but become unfruitful? Or will they become an avid seed-sower themselves, multiplying faith to hundreds and thousands of others? We do not know for sure, so we share with anyone and everyone.

However, if the seed is never cast, it will not matter what kind of soil the people are.

Where must we go to find soil that has never once received seed sown upon its surface? Where are there people living completely unreached by the gospel of Jesus?

BIRTH OF THE FINAL 58

"**H**ow many tribes are there in Laos?"

It was 1999 and I was spending the summer in the northern city of Luang Prabang leading a team of missionary interns. We found a young couple residing in town who operated a small business. I posed my question to the husband because I wanted to learn all that he could tell me.

"About ten, I'd say," was his reply, unaware that there were many more. At the time, we had a list of more than 100 people groups listed for Laos. Traditionally, the Lao government lumped them together into three groups— Lowland, Upland and Highland Lao, based upon their traditional living spaces in the mountains and valleys. Later on the government acknowledged around forty distinct ethnicities in the country. A few foreign surveyors, however, were finding many more.

"We have a list of almost 140 groups," I reported. The man was dumbfounded. Never had he heard there were so many. In fact, it wasn't believable to him. *How could there be so many? Where are they?* Even if you were to ask a Lao person who was born and raised in a northern province of Laos where there is the greatest diversity, he or she still might tell you that there are only three tribes or perhaps up to a dozen.

Sometimes called "hidden groups," unique tribal communities persist in regions of the world that possess the right ingredients for cultural and linguistic diversification. Some of these ingredients are steep mountain ranges, lack of infrastructure, border regions, and underdeveloped systems of government. These features contribute to the separation and isolation of groups, who then develop their own dialects, cultures, and ethnic identities. This precisely describes the situation in much of the remote areas of Laos. Consequently, there are a vast number of unique ethnic communities that even Lao urban dwellers, the Lowland Lao, are unaware. More often than not, when a Lowland Lao person encounters someone from an unknown tribe, they lump him or her together with a larger, more familiar minority. They are combined with others in spite of unique languages, customs, and identity. In this way, distinct groups remain hidden under their noses.

A HIDDEN PEOPLE

"Ouch!" I blurted. The dog bit me in the calf. Thankfully, he did not draw blood. I was standing high in the mountains of Phongsali province, near the border of China, trying to communicate with some tribal men who did not speak any Lao. We met them as we hiked along the path after a fallen tree prevented our truck from going any further. I had to draw pictures on a scrap of paper to convey words, and as I did, I inadvertently stepped on the tail of the dog accompanying the mountain men.

"They don't even know how to say *khop chai* in Lao!" I marveled to my partner, Travis, who had just moved to Laos and accompanied me on this trip north. *Khop chai* means "thank you" in Lao. I was amazed that these tribal people, living inside the national borders of Laos, did not know this phrase. Even foreigners learn to say *khop chai* on their first day in the country. They did, however, know the word *laengz zingh*—the Mien words for "thank you."

Travis and I were on the hunt for uncharted Mien villages. Neither of us had ever visited Phongsali before, and we were excited to forge into new territory. I had heard there were Mien in Phongsali province. However, I had also heard there were Lanten people too. The Lanten are a tribal group that is very similar to the Mien, yet distinct. Their languages are related, but separate. The government usually lumped them together under one tribal identifier: the Yao.

Together with my Lao partners, we had already done the painstaking work of visiting every Mien village in the other provinces of northern Laos to distinguish which ones were Mien, which ones were Lanten, and which (very few) had both. With the use of portable GPS units, we were able to mark the coordinates of all the Mien villages in Laos, besides Phongsali province. Phongsali was still uncharted territory. We had a list of more than twenty Yao villages, but we didn't know which ones were Mien and which ones were Lanten. Travis and I were there to sort it out.

We discovered something we never expected: a new people group.

Existing maps of the roads and villages of Laos are unreliable, at best. We found that we could get a much better idea of locations by looking at Google Earth and zooming down close enough to see jungle roads and rooftops. Along with some unreliable maps, Travis and I used this method to find some of the first Yao villages in Phongsali province. Excavators had originally cut pathways off the main highways to reach some of the villages, but creeping jungles of vines, weeds and trees had since reclaimed them. Travis and I made our way down one such path with my four-wheel drive truck only to come to the aforementioned fallen tree. Even turning around was going to be difficult—there was a mountain wall on one side of the roadway and a steep cliff on the other.

Encountering the tree was disheartening. From the look of the map, we were still about two kilometers away from the village. We decided to hike the rest of the way. We had come too far to give up now. Down in the valley below lay two or three of these Yao villages, and a quick visit would tell us what we needed to know.

We did not have to go too far, however, when we met the contingent of men and their dog walking up the pathway. A few of them carried handmade muskets. They were on a hunting trip and were startled to see two white men so far out in the mountains but kind enough to give communication a shot.

One of the young men actually knew a few Thai words, even though he could not speak Lao. He undoubtedly picked this up from Thai television broadcasts. Even in remote villages, many people will get a small TV and a cheap Chinese satellite dish to pick up a reception. It seems strange to first-time visitors to Laos but is actually quite common.

Through Thai, a little of the Mien language I spoke, and pictures I drew, we were able to have basic communication. Their word for "thank you" was the same as the Mien, even though the Lanten people use a different expression. A picture of a house I drew elicited the word *biauv*, also the same as Mien. Chicken, however, was different in their language—not the same as the Mien term. I played an audio recording of the Mien language, spoken by a Mien person, and they could not understand it.

The young man was familiar with the Lanten of Luang Nam Tha province and insisted they were not the same. He did not know the word Mien at all, and when I showed him a picture of a Mien woman dressed in traditional clothing, he and his friends insisted that she was "not Yao." Their clothing looked much more similar to the Lanten than the Mien. But I knew enough about the term "Yao" to know it was an *exonym* (a name that outsiders call a people group) and not an *endonym* (the name a people group uses to call itself, often meaning just "people" in their own language). I pressed him on what they call themselves, and it finally came out that they called themselves the Moon people.

In all likelihood, the Moon people are more closely related to the Lanten people (whose endonym is the Kim Mun) than the Mien. However, it was interesting to see that some of their language terms were the same as the Mien rather than the Lanten (e.g. *thank you*) and that they were familiar with the Lanten of Luang Nam Tha and insisted they were distinct groups. More ethnographic study would need to be conducted to come to a precise classification, but the Moon people of Phongsali were clearly a group related to both the Lanten and Mien (under the Yao umbrella) yet distinct in their own right. Outsiders who had previously classified them lumped them together with other Yao people, so even though they were a sizeable group for the region, they were a hidden people. They were a good example of a hidden and completely unreached people group that had never been engaged with the gospel message of Jesus Christ.

BIRTH OF A VISION

In 2017, I was approached with a proposal to do something about all the tribes in Laos that remained completely unreached and never engaged with a gospel-sharing mission. The largest and most accessible people groups in Laos had already been engaged with the gospel, and a few were even reached by some definitions. But now I was looking specifically at the people groups that had never had a sustained effort to reach them with Christ's message. We had a list of 58 such groups for Laos. *What would it take to reach them all?*

The wheels started turning. I began to pray and seek God's direction. I decided to approach this effort from the basis of abundance, rather than poverty. Often, when we make plans that have huge hopes we look at our own resources (or lack of them, I should say) and ask ourselves, *What can I do with what I have right now?* We certainly do this in regards to finances but also with time and human resources. We forget that God owns everything and the cattle on a thousand hills, and even ten million dollars is small change for him.

In fact, God could raise up an army from a valley of dry bones if he wanted. So, I determined to have faith—not to plan based on what I thought I could realistically do in my own power, but as if God said to me, "All my money and resources are at your disposal, Eliot. How will you go about this?"

Have you ever dreamed what you would do with a million dollars? This was my approach. Immediately two things became clear to me: we need a survey to find and confirm the existence and location of these small people groups, and we need to mobilize Lao Christians for this task, not Western missionaries. Because these unengaged and unreached people groups were so small and remote, it would make much more sense for Lao Christians from other tribes to share the good news with them than to figure out ways to recruit sixty more expatriate missionaries from the West. This approach would also help to strengthen the Lao church. Like Abraham in Genesis 12, they would be blessed to be a blessing to others and grow to become more like God in the process.

The next question was from where we would recruit these national missionaries, as I began to call them. God then brought to my mind a number of missionaries around the country, from north to south, who had a heart for reaching the unreached. The idea began to develop that we could partner with different missionaries in each region, along with local Lao churches, to recruit, train, and mobilize national missionaries to the unengaged unreached people groups in their corresponding regions. Since the fifty-eight groups were scattered throughout the country, this approach made sense. My next step was to cast the vision to these potential partners.

"Sorry, I like your idea, Eliot, but I'm just already too busy with what I'm doing." I started to hear this sentiment often from some great people. "It sounds great, but I am still trying to reach my specific unreached people group. I need to stay focused on it," was another. I understood these responses, though others were more wary of the idea. "Wouldn't it be better just to train the existing Lao church leaders, and eventually the gospel will reach these groups?" One more objected, "I don't think I agree with compensating Lao nationals to do ministry—it's just setting up dependency." These were the sentiments, if not the quotes.

None of my friends categorically opposed the plan, though there were varying levels of support for the idea. It was clear that I must make the case for both *intentionality*—specifically targeting these unengaged unreached people groups and mobilizing workers to each one—and for *compensation*—

using outside resources to support local efforts in a way that did not create dependency or exacerbate money and ministry issues, which abound in places like Laos.

I did not have much faith in the "trickle down" theory of evangelism. This is the idea that if we win those in the majority, those with wealth and influence, then it will eventually reach the smaller and more remote groups. It does happen on occasion, but throughout history, hidden groups have remained so for a reason—cultural, linguistic, social, and physical barriers have proven to isolate them from the reach of the gospel. Even if Christianity completely saturated the surrounding tribes, it still might not make the jump to the hidden group. "Trickle down" was not going to get the job done any time soon. An intentional effort to target each group was needed.

Compensation was a bit trickier. Countless well-intentioned Christian visitors to Laos desire to make a difference, find a local partner who seems agreeable, and sponsor him or her to do ministry. Frequently, this does not turn out well. Waving a pile of money around and asking for volunteers to come take it is a sure way to draw out many of the wrong people with impure motives.

I'll never forget the story a missionary in Thailand told me from a previous generation. He was visiting a remote northern city where he met a Chinese-Thai man. When the man learned that my friend was a missionary, he immediately volunteered to be his evangelist. "I will go and preach anywhere you want me to go! I will start churches, and I will do all of the work for you! All you have to do is pay me a salary, and I'll get the job done!" My missionary friend was intrigued but wanted to know about his experience. "How long have you been a Christian?" he asked the man. "Oh, I am not a Christian," the Chinese-Thai man answered, "but that's no problem—you just tell me what to teach and I will teach it!" My missionary friend declined, though he did implore him to turn to Christ himself.

I only wanted to recruit Lao Christians who genuinely knew and loved God and had a heart to share him with unreached tribes. Only God truly knows peoples' hearts, but a good sign that a person was sincere was if they had a history of sharing Jesus without any compensation for their efforts. It was the surest indication of sincerity and potential for a good partnership. I knew it was important to find people who demonstrated faithfulness and fruitfulness in their walk when it was not accompanied by any financial compensation or physical benefit. This would help address the pitfall of recruiting the wrong kind of people. But what about creating dependency?

Dependency is a huge problem in poor countries where missionaries from wealthy nations go to serve. It is easy to install pipelines of financial resources to sustain ongoing ministry efforts. Missionaries (both short- and long-term) have supported the salaries of pastors, built church buildings, and funded programs indefinitely. The local churches and pastors become accustomed to this support and rely upon it. Pastors' salaries grow far beyond the level of the church members, and the church's expenses exceed the amount they would gather even if every member gave a double tithe of their income. It is not sustainable, and whenever the source of outside funds shuts off, the ministry and church collapse.

The last thing I wanted to do was to construct a system of dependency! Consequently, it was important to make a clear distinction between what we called a national missionary and a national pastor. A national pastor was a Lao person leading and shepherding his church, of his own tribe or ethnic group, in an ongoing fashion. A national missionary, on the other hand, is a Lao person who crosses cultures to introduce the gospel to a new unreached tribe that has never heard it before. The national missionary does the work of a missionary, not the work of a pastor. A national missionary's role is temporary—to make disciples, establish the church, and equip the locals to lead and pastor their own people without any reliance upon outside funds. When a sustainable and multiplying church is established and capable believers are appointed to shepherd and lead, the national missionary leaves. This is the essential difference. Much like missionaries from the West who enjoy the support of people in their home countries to serve in Laos, these Lao national missionaries would be supported from the outside to work cross-culturally in yet unreached tribes. They may not be fully supported from their own home churches, but they could be supported by the larger global church to complete the task God has given to all of us. Most importantly, none of their funds is used to support the ministry of new believers in the tribes they reach—they establish simple churches appropriate for the level of resources the local believers have at their own disposal.

I knew I must cast the vision appropriately or I would not be able to find any willing partners. Then God led me to Nick.

I had been acquainted with Nick for years but never got to know him very well. Like myself, he had long experience running large projects in Laos and managing Lao people but in a distant province from where I lived. He was fluent in the Lao language and had already gone through the learning curve of mistakes made and problems faced while working in Laos with other expatriates and nationals. I bought a plane ticket on the last flight in and out of his remote city to visit him before the rainy season shut everything down.

Nick and I talked for hours as I laid the entire vision out before him and we shared our histories with each other. We were heartened to find that we had separately arrived at many of the same ideas and opinions about how to work effectively in Laos after having gone through so many challenges. This became the basis of a good relationship of trust and mutual respect.

Nick was intrigued by the prospect of mobilizing equipped Lao national missionaries to specific unengaged unreached people groups throughout the country, rather than just targeting the dark places around him. Like me, he had a desire to reach all the tribes in Laos. Nick agreed that a survey would be needed to confirm the outdated and unreliable data we had on these fifty-eight groups. Still, he did not yet bite on the idea. Neither did I want him to. I wanted him to pray and to be led by God, not persuaded by my words.

Over the next few months, as he prayed, God laid these final fifty-eight unengaged unreached people groups in Laos on Nick's heart. He knew he was in a position to do something about it and to manage the effort. Nick's vision, however, was not just for his region of the country—he wanted to mobilize workers to all the unreached tribes remaining in the entire country of Laos. In light of the unavailability of other potential partners, Nick was just what I needed!

The seed had been planted. Now, the vision was born! Together we would develop an effort to reach all the tribes in Laos that had not yet been given the opportunity to know and turn to Jesus.

In January 2018, Nick and I met in Chiang Mai, Thailand, to hash out the structure and plan for what we were now calling the Final 58. A group of about ten missionaries joining the Final 58 effort assembled there to develop the plan. This included American, Thai, British, Korean, and Lao partners, most of them from different mission organizations. Pastor Woun, the Hmong pastor from Xieng Khuang (who would later invite me to conduct the recruitment training at his home church where my passport was confiscated) was there to help put this entire strategy together. Experienced missionaries from other fields, who were not joining the Final 58 team, gathered with us to offer their insight and experience.

By the end of our time together, we had listed every potential partner available to us in the country of Laos, discussed how best to partner with the official Lao Evangelical Church, described pitfalls and challenges, and laid the framework for what would become one of the most unique and exciting mission efforts the world has ever seen. At these early stages, however, all we had was faith. We had no idea about all that God was about to do. As I have related to others the stories you will read in the following chapters, more than a few have made the same remark:

"That sounds like the book of Acts!"

FAITH JOURNEY

Woosh! *Woosh!* Two fighter jets flew overhead, maneuvering a sharp turn at low altitude. Since relocating to Virginia Beach a few months before I moved to Laos in 2001, I had noticed regular fighter jet activity in the skies above. I was there to share about the work I would be doing in Laos with a supporting church and to cast vision for missions involvement. The fighter jets were an unexpected (and cool!) bonus to my time in the city.

Virginia Beach is known for its military base and community. It wasn't long before I noticed that the fighter jets were conducting the same maneuvers repeatedly. I asked a friend who had formerly served in the Navy what they were doing.

"They are playing war games. In the military, they create highly stressful wartime scenarios. Suppose the enemy has knocked out certain communications or other capabilities have been compromised. In these moments, you have to successfully navigate the situation and practice the right procedures with limited ability." My friend was happy to enlighten a novice. "Everyone will tell you—the war games are much more difficult than real war!"

"Why is that?" I asked.

"They design it to be that way. They want our soldiers to be prepared for the absolute worst. So, they train them with the most difficult scenarios possible. Then, when they go to war for real, it seems almost easy." A smirk of pride broke across his face at the expression of our nation's military prowess.

Years later, I remembered this conversation as we considered how we might train Lao Christians to serve as national missionaries. How might we apply this principle in the Final 58?

For many Lao Christians, the idea of becoming a servant of God does not mean a humble existence enduring hardship. On the contrary, it is more akin to what James and John had requested of Jesus—to serve him on his right and his left when he ascended to his throne. They didn't ask to become king themselves (they allowed Jesus to keep that honor). They just wanted to be #2 and #3 in the nation—servants to Jesus but honored and exalted above everyone else. In the old days of the Lao monarchy, the Lao kings had numerous servants who closely associated with the king, serving his wishes but also enjoying a life of honor and privilege as royal officials. Consequently, becoming a pastor, church leader, or otherwise "servant" of God in Laos did not come with the connotation of humility but with the expectation of being revered and respected as a religious leader.

The Lao missionaries we hoped to send out, however, would never enjoy this kind of luxury in their role. On the contrary, they would be traveling to some of the most remote corners of the country, over treacherous roads, in terrible conditions, working with some of the lowest people on the social hierarchy, and facing potential arrest, torture, and imprisonment for daring to forge new territory with the gospel. Becoming a Final 58 national missionary would not be the path to high regard. Therefore, we needed to recruit the right people and then find a way to train them appropriately. The danger of sending them out unprepared to thrive in the field could backfire. It would create a backlash so severe that few others would ever want to join the effort after learning what they would face. But how could we prepare them?

How did Jesus prepare his disciples?

After choosing twelve men who had not attended Pharisee school, Jesus took his group of fishermen, tax collectors, and a zealot around with him for three years. He modeled to them his method for announcing the good news to the poor, offering freedom for the oppressed, healing for the sick and sight for the blind, and proclaiming the year of the Lord's favor. He taught his disciples privately, and they listened to him teach the masses. He shared countless stories with them to shift their paradigms. Finally, he also sent them out on short-term trips to repeat his process.

What was the biggest thing the disciples needed to learn to serve him effectively? Time and again, it was the following: they must learn to truly have faith.

With faith they would not have to worry about food or clothes.
With faith they would be safe from the storms.

With faith they would be forgiven and healed.

With faith they would withstand harsh persecution.

With faith they would see miracles.

With faith they would walk on water.

With faith they would drive out demons.

With faith they would move mountains.

With faith they would pray and receive what they asked for.

With faith they would be saved.

With faith they would gain eternal life.

With faith they would receive the Holy Spirit.

With faith they would be given greater responsibility.

With faith they would overcome worry.

With faith they would see the glory of God.

With faith they would do the same things Jesus did and even greater things.

With faith anything would be possible for them.

Often, Jesus pleaded with his disciples: *Where is your faith?*

Faith is like a muscle. The only way to grow it is to use it. The Lao brothers and sisters we were preparing to mobilize would carry the gospel message of Jesus to unreached tribes in remote locations of Laos. Teaching them that they *can* rely upon God to do this would never help them grow in their reliance upon God until they *actually relied* upon him. Serving God while relying on our own ability, resources, and wisdom does not allow much room for God to come through for us. Unfortunately, this mode of serving out of our flesh is all too common. Serving out of faith, however, fully depends upon God to bring the success.

In Judges 7, Gideon assembled his army to fight the Midianites when God said to him, "Your army is too big. I can't let you win with this many soldiers. The Israelites would think that they had won the battle all by themselves and that I didn't have anything to do with it" (Judges 7:2-3, CEV). God pared his army down from thirty-two thousand men to a mere three hundred. It took extreme faith in God by Gideon and his three hundred men even to think about approaching the enemy. In the end, only a miracle would save them, and that is exactly what God delivered. They won not because they were so powerful, talented, or well equipped—they won because they had genuine faith in God to do for them what they never could have accomplished on their own.

In a similar fashion, Jesus sent out seventy-two of his disciples in Luke 10 to do ministry without Jesus being right there with them. Instead of setting them up with all the money, food, and resources they needed, he told them:

> Don't take along a moneybag or a traveling bag or sandals. And don't waste time greeting people on the road. As soon as you enter a home, say, "God bless this home with peace." If the people living there are peace-loving, your prayer for peace will bless them. But if they are not peace-loving, your prayer will return to you. Stay with the same family, eating and drinking whatever they give you, because workers are worth what they earn. Don't move around from house to house. If the people of a town welcome you, eat whatever they offer. Heal their sick and say, "God's kingdom will soon be here!" (Luke 10:4-9, CEV).

Jesus's instructions to the seventy-two were to accomplish his mission (preaching, praying, and healing) relying completely upon the hospitality offered to them by those who received them in the unreached towns. His filter for finding someone to bless was someone who would have pity on them and shelter and feed them. In this way, they would see God's hand in action. And it worked! When the seventy-two returned to Jesus, they were excited about what had happened. They exercised their faith, and their faith increased. Their faith muscle became stronger.

Nick had an idea on how to train our Lao national missionaries in the same way. He shared his idea with me, and I absolutely loved it. Taking Luke 10 as our model, we would send out all our recruits to remote unreached villages on what we would call a faith journey. The faith journey would begin with several days of study on Luke 10, an explanation of the purpose and process of what we were doing, and then five full days in the field. Participants would bring only enough money with them for a bus ticket home—no charging cords for their phones, no food, and no change of clothes. We would put them on a bus to a predetermined region, and from there they would walk to their target area. They could accept rides, food, and shelter from anyone who offered, but they would not ask for it. Instead, they would pray and ask God to lead them to the people he wanted them to encounter. They would announce God's kingdom, share a simple gospel message they had practiced, seek to bless anyone they met, and pray for healing for anyone who was ailing. They would go from house to house until someone invited them in and then stay there. If a village did not welcome them, they would shake the dust off their shoes and walk to the next village. If no one accepted them, they would sleep in the jungle or an abandoned field house. After five full days on the field, they would return home.

We decided to give it a try. Nick accompanied the first group out into the field. The following is his report of his experience with his partner, Choy:

We landed in the northernmost district of the northernmost province in Laos—into a sea of diverse tribes and languages. It was about an hour until dusk when we got off the bus, and we still had a five-to-six kilometer hike ahead of us. It took longer than expected, and night fell while we were still on the road. We were expectant of what might happen but also fearful that we would not be welcomed in the village after dark. We wondered if we would spend our first night outside in a field house in the middle of a rice paddy. The thought wasn't so appealing as the number of mosquitos buzzing around increased.

We made it to a village, however, with no regular electricity. Many of the homes were lit with dim lamps powered by batteries charged with solar panels. We descended the slope into the village and heard unintelligible voices off to the left. We approached the first house and met a family standing around outside. "Hello," I said, "we've just walked here from the last village. We've come to visit, to pray, and to bless you." The family responded positively, and within a few minutes, we were whisked inside a genuine Akha Kor home.

It seemed quite late. We had finished a delicious, but strange, meal and had shared the gospel message with a number of young men who joined us. "We know what you say is the truth," admitted one man. "The elders in the village have shared similar things." We marveled at how God prepares hearts even when the village worships spirits. That night we slept hard.

Early the next morning, our hosts treated Choy and me to a good Akha breakfast—pickled mystery root and rice. We departed with light hearts and a spring in our step. We offered prayers, songs, and thanksgiving all along the winding trail ahead of us.

Several hours later, we arrived at the next small village. It was still mid-morning. Besides a few kids and some lumbering pigs and pecking chickens, the village was quiet. Most everyone had gone to work in the fields. We decided to try to visit this village again when we returned.

By the time we reached the next village, it was almost noon. We took a few moments to pray before proceeding. Entering the village required scaling a ladder up a steep incline. At the top, a Lolo man was sitting in front of his home. "Hello!" we greeted him. "We've walked from the Akha village. We've come to pray, bless, and share stories." As we talked, we shared the good news and blessed this man in Jesus's name. He gave us water and invited us inside for a meal.

Later, as we continued our journey, I began to wonder what Jesus meant in Luke 10:9 (NIV): "Heal the sick who are there and tell them, 'The kingdom of God has come near to you.'" Earlier, I discounted saying this, reasoning that no one in these villages would have a clue about the kingdom of God. Then it dawned upon me that in Jesus's time, people didn't understand about the kingdom either. Yet, Jesus still made this central to his training.

Just then, a man drove his motorbike down the trail in the same direction we were headed. He stopped and inquired, "Where are you going?" "To the next village," I replied. "We are here because the kingdom of God has come near. We've come to pray, to bless, and to exchange stories." To be honest, I felt a bit foolish saying this, but the man responded simply by saying, "Great. Come visit me tonight." After giving us his name and village, he continued down the dusty trail.

"Wow!" I thought. "That was cool and easy. Maybe there is something to this."

We were still learning. We kept forgetting to follow Jesus's instruction in Luke 10:5 (NIV): "When you enter a house, first say, 'Peace to this house!'" Even in my conversation with the man on the motorcycle, I had forgotten his instruction to "greet no one along the road."

As Choy and I walked into the last village for the day, we found ourselves surrounded by yet another unreached people group—the Haw. After the first two houses refused us, Choy suggested we shake the dust from our feet and be on our way. However, we persisted, looking for a man working or sitting outside of a house. This had become our usual practice.

Upon hearing some voices, we followed the trail up to a house that had several men sitting in front of it. All of these men spoke decent Lao, and we quickly introduced our mission. "We've come because the kingdom of God is near." We blessed them in the name of Jesus, and since they didn't have sickness to pray for, we proceeded to share the gospel message.

The men turned out to be good hosts and fed us a fabulous meal. At first, there was no invitation to stay for the night. As we were getting up from dinner to head out though, they asked about lodging and invited us to stay with them. We gratefully accepted.

Early the next morning we embarked on a ten-kilometer hike up a mountain to the next village. At one high point along the way, we found a spot with cell phone reception. Text messages lit up our phone, and we learned that another one of our teams out on their faith journey had been arrested! My heart was heavy, and for a few hours, I fretted about them and all the other teams. I became worried about our business platform, and my family being able to stay in Laos. Thankfully, within a few hours, I dealt with these worries in my heart, and we continued on in faith.

Choy, my Lao partner on this faith journey, was a refreshing example of gratitude. When the sun was shining, he would say, "Thank you Lord for keeping the path clear of mud." When it rained, he was thankful that the sun's rays were tempered and the air was cool.

As we approached the next village, we encountered a man resting in his hillside shelter and sat with him. Choy had been practicing his gospel presentation during the hike. He eagerly took the opportunity to share with this Akha man. He didn't get far, however, until it became clear that the man was unable to comprehend what he said. Many Akha villagers do not speak Lao. Determined, Choy continued his whole presentation with the man for the sake of practice.

We found the tribal people's inability to speak Lao very frustrating. It was difficult to tell how much the people understood of what we shared. As we climbed up the rest of the way into the village, we prayed for the Lord to guide us and for those to whom he would lead us.

Person after person in this Akha Kor village could not speak Lao. We ambled through the village until we spied an old man sitting in front of his house. His ability to speak Lao wasn't much better, but he called a friend to come listen. As we shared the gospel, a number of others trickled into the house, but only one of them could understand.

"No, we can never leave the spirits!" the man repeated emphatically. He refused to listen to the remainder of the story. We had been welcomed into the house and provided a meal and water to drink. Suddenly, the welcome became stale. It was 2 p.m., but we felt it was time for us to leave. We considered looking for another house in the village (and hoping someone would be able to communicate with us), but remembered Jesus's command that after entering a household not to go from house to house but to stay there until leaving the village. So, we went on our way.

As it turned out, this mountaintop village was indeed the end of the road for all motorized transport. However, there was an infrequently traveled jungle trail leading out of the village. The villagers told us that it led to another village just six kilometers from the district city.

"Let's do it!"

Choy, a young man of 25, and myself (not so young) should be able to do it. Or so we thought. The villagers said that it took just four hours but that we would cross three or four mountains before finding the bigger trail to the next village.

As we passed the last house in the Akha mountaintop village, rain began to fall. The steep trail led down a mountainside. Several trails branched off, and we wondered which branch we should take. We decided upon the muddy trail littered with decaying leaves. The grasses and bushes encroached upon the trail such that it took great concentration not to miss the trail entirely and get off track.

Choy was leading the way when he stopped suddenly, grabbed a stick, and started yelling. "We can step on snakes and scorpions!" However, rather than step, he decided to whack a serpent lying along the path. *Whack, whack, whack*! The deed was done. We proceeded down the mountain, undeterred.

A bit further down the trail I noticed something unusual. There was movement on the trail around our feet. It appeared that the trail itself was moving. Thin, black, tree leeches, about two-to-three inches long, covered the forest floor. They would alternately make a beeline (leeches are quick!) for our feet or would wildly wave their heads around trying to discern the right direction to head. Later, we learned that leeches are covered with receptors that detect odors, vibrations, and body heat. They can also sense increased carbon dioxide in the air put off by humans and animals. All these things help the leeches find their next meal!

Soon, we were running wildly through the jungle in a desperate effort to minimize exposure to the leeches. We weren't successful. Every twenty yards or so, we stopped to pull off the gobs of leeches accumulating on our legs. They still managed to find us, despite our light-footedness. I guess we ran for more than an hour in our attempt to avoid the leeches and pulled off too many to count.

Several mountains later, with the leeches finally behind us, we found ourselves in a secret opium field. Then it happened—somehow we had lost the trail. Before us was a mountain covered in thick jungle. Choy, who had bravely led the way from the beginning, offered to cut a new trail. However, we lacked any good machete or sharp tool. We did our best to make do.

Walking was impossible. We ascended the mountainside by crawling, and it was quite challenging. The foliage was so thick and the terrain so convoluted that I could not even see Choy, though he was but twenty or so feet ahead. "Choy, where are you?" I repeatedly yelled. I'd hear the sound of his answer and pull myself in his direction.

Vines seemed to have fingers, grabbing and pulling at our legs and feet. It was like trying continually to escape a giant net. Many of the vines had razor sharp thorns. Our sandals were utterly useless in the spongy mix of mud, grass, and leaves on the forest floor, so I went barefoot. The thorns cut my feet, and the vines held their grasp. At this point, my trust in the Lord faltered. "This is so stupid!" I bellowed more than once. Nightfall was approaching fast, and we were stuck in the middle of a vast jungle.

At one point, I slithered into a pit so deep I couldn't escape. Choy, more nimble than me, graciously pulled me up and out over stinging nettles. On we traveled until we finally found a trail. We proceeded to run down the path in a final effort to beat the darkness. We arrived at an Akha village just as night fell.

It was a mixed reception. We joined a large dinner party complete with exotic Akha foods, and they quickly invited us to stay the night. Our attempts to share the gospel, however, were thwarted. The prominent man who could speak Lao changed his tune. Now he spoke strongly, warning us that it was against the Lao nation to believe in Jesus. He shared how they had fined and expelled others who had once brought the message of Jesus into the village. An older man spoke very unkindly to us. Then, another man yelled loudly and made threats. The host himself changed his countenance toward us and became rather rude. It was quite a turn. The next morning, the host refused to see us off, and we left early. If there was a time to shake the dust from our feet, this was it. And so we did.

It turned out that the intelligence from the day before was a bit inaccurate. It wasn't six kilometers to the district town from this village; it was over thirty. Still, this was the shortest distance between two points. Given our options, we decided to make the most of it. We forged ahead.

By noon, we had covered sixteen kilometers of mountainous jungle road. Finally, we found ourselves at the paved road. There also happened to be a village at the bottom of the hill. Would they receive us?

It was a Keu village—one of just two or three Keu villages in all of Laos. The first couple of men we spoke to listened politely but were not receptive. The next household was even less open. It was unclear how much Lao they understood. I suspected this might be another village to shake the dust from our feet. We were weary, thirsty, and hungry, and I was losing hope of receiving any sort of positive reception. Just then, a thin, old wrinkled man waved at us from the balcony of his stilted house. "Come on up!"

"This is a waste of time," I thought. "This man won't be able to speak any Lao." Despite my misgivings, we remembered to ask for peace to rest upon this house as we ascended the stairs. We didn't bother with much small talk but just started giving him blessings. In response, the man asked for prayers of healing, then for more prayer, and then for even more. His wife requested prayers for healing as well. We obliged.

We were exhausted from our trek through the jungle. After praying, we simply sat and rested on his balcony. It had been a long hike and we were without water. We could have requested it but had set ourselves to ask only from the Lord. So, we just sat there parched. Quietly, I prayed, "Lord please give us some water." Almost immediately, the old man jumped up with unlikely vigor. He ran into the next room and quickly returned carrying a water pot and two glasses. *Thank you, God!*

"That prayer worked nicely," I thought. So, I tried again, "Lord, please give us something to eat." Again, the man jumped up appearing stirred and excited. "Mangos!" he exclaimed, nearly too quickly to be understood. "Mangos! We have mangos!" In a few minutes, he had knocked down three green mangos from his tree, and we were feasting on salt and pepper and green mangos. *Thank you, Jesus!* The family also invited us to stay the night. We praised God for such good hosts!

The next morning, we continued our journey full of joy. The Lord had taken us through Akha Kor, LoLo, more Akha Kor, Keu, and Thai Leu villages. At every step, the Lord supplied us abundantly. He had taken care of both big concerns and small. He had given us trials and testing but had also prepared the hearts of many villagers to hear the name of Jesus for the very first time. He also taught us to ask only from the Lord, to trust in him, and not to rely upon our own resources and ways. He proved that he was reliable.

We made it back home close to midnight—and fell into a good sleep.

The team that the police had detained spent several days in jail and under house arrest at a guesthouse. One of them, a young man named Tawee, wanted to see if others had been arrested and how he could help. He escaped, leaving his partner behind, and hitchhiked all the way back to the provincial capital. Confusion set in regarding what had happened, but later Tawee was able to return to rescue his partner without having to pay any bribes to the police.

All the teams safely returned from the Final 58's first faith journey. During debrief, we discovered that many of them faced language barriers and people who were not hospitable. Several of them were brought in for questioning by village authorities but later released when they were deemed not to be a threat. Others were welcomed in, and many who had never heard about Jesus before listened to the gospel for the first time. One team led two people to faith in Christ!

We also discovered that several of them faltered, relying upon money and food they had secretly brought with them or by directly asking others for food and housing. Even so, it was still an extremely valuable training in practicing faith while serving God's mission. All of them saw that God would indeed provide for them and that they were able to serve God without being loaded to the hilt with money, food, and transportation.

When Peter saw Jesus walking on water, his first impulse was to ask to walk on water too. How happy this must have made Jesus! Peter was not only witnessing an impossible miracle, but he also asked to do the same. After a few steps, he faltered and began to sink. The other disciples, who never dared venture over the edge of the boat, may have looked upon Peter's lack of faith as a failure. Even so, it was still an extremely valuable training in practicing and growing his faith. Peter flexed his faith muscle. He faltered, yet he grew.

The Faith Journey has now become a rite of passage for all of the Lao national missionaries who have entered our training program. Before finishing their five-month Boot Camp training, they must complete a five-day Faith Journey in the field, relying only upon God and the hospitality of strangers with whom they share the gospel. In this way, God has prepared our Lao national missionaries to walk by faith. Not by might, and not by power, but by the Spirit of the Lord they have stepped out in faith to proffer Christ's hope to those in darkness.

Would this faith be enough to bear fruit for God's kingdom?

FIRSTFRUITS

THE LAOSENG

Teo and Boonmi rode their motorbike up the winding dirt road into the mountains. They were on the hunt for a tribe called the Laoseng. Teo and Boonmi had already visited countless villages in some of the most remote corners of Laos to survey tribes the world had never known to exist. They were part of our initial survey effort for the Final 58. Earlier in the year, I had spent time with the survey team explaining the challenges of finding and confirming groups on our list and sorting out their names. We were venturing out into new territory and wanted to be careful yet not pass up gospel opportunities.

After traveling more than eighty kilometers from the urban center, Teo and Boonmi arrived at Sukan village, at the very end of the road. Sukan was situated on the border with Vietnam. The Laoseng people who lived there were strange and spoke a unique language. Because of their remote location, they did not speak Lao. Teo and Boonmi wondered how they would communicate with the Laoseng people and gather information. They prayed and trusted that God would provide a way.

The Laoseng both grow and use opium. Teo and Boonmi observed many people in the village suffering the consequences of their addiction. Like most remote tribal groups, the Laoseng are also animists—gripped by fear that the spirits will cause them to suffer in sickness or poverty. Therefore, they placate the spirits with offerings. Despite this, the Laoseng still endure much adversity. Spirit worship does not seem to help.

Teo and Boonmi searched for the village headman but learned that he was not home. Instead, they were pleased to meet an older Laoseng woman named Nang. Nang was unique in the village because she could speak Lao in addition to the Laoseng language. Teo and Boonmi thanked God for leading them to her. As a Lao speaker, Nang served as an important government liaison and leader in the village. Teo and Boonmi decided to gather the survey information from her.

"Are you poor or happy? How is life here in this village?" they asked. Nang mentioned all the problems, sickness, and opium usage there. Boonmi asked her, "How do you think we can overcome all of these problems?" Nang did not have an answer. She knew what they were doing was not working. She just did not know of any other way. The spirits kept them poor, sick, and filled with sadness, but *what else should they do?* Nang said, "Usually we just feed the spirits, but we're not sure if the spirits can really save us."

Teo and Boonmi took this opportunity to share with Nang about Jesus, the One who can really save. Boonmi explained the source of problems in the world as coming from sin and not knowing our Creator and Father. "There are two kinds of problems," he said, "physical and spiritual problems. God is over everything, and nothing in this world can save us except Jesus." Nang was interested.

From this point, Teo and Boonmi shared the Creation-to-Christ story with Nang. They explained how Jesus came down into the world, how he lived and died, and that one day he will come again. After sharing the gospel with Nang, she decided that she wanted to become a follower of Jesus. Teo and Boonmi prayed with her to receive Christ.

Immediately after receiving Christ, Nang called her husband and children inside to hear the story. She wanted them to know about God—about what she had just learned. Teo and Boonmi took time to share the gospel and explain to Nang's husband and children too. Together, they all decided to place their faith in Christ!

In the history of the world, the Laoseng people have never believed or even heard the gospel. They have been completely disconnected, living in darkness in one of the most remote places on earth and in submission to evil spirits who do not have their best interests at heart. We were delighted that even during the survey phase of the Final 58 effort, our Lao partners were able to share the gospel with these unreached people.

MUSHROOM

When we began the survey, we fully expected that some of the groups on the list of 58 would not exist or would remain unfound. We thought that the

Final 58 might end up being the Final 35 before we began the engagement phase in earnest, when we would mobilize our national missionaries to share the gospel and make disciples among the groups we had confirmed. What we found, however, was that the opposite was true.

Instead of crossing names off the list, the number of unengaged unreached people groups in Laos actually mushroomed as we continued to discover more and more hidden tribes. Our list of 58 grew to 158, with 96 of those groups being confirmed. To confirm a group, we needed to be able to mark its location and determine its name at a minimum. After the survey phase was completed, some of the original 58 were found to be engaged already, a few with thriving churches. Other groups on the list remained unconfirmed—we failed to locate or confirm their existence at all.

We quickly realized that survey work could consume multiple lifetimes of ethnographic research to sort out misinformation, find missing groups, or determine levels of ethnic and linguistic distinction. We felt strongly that the groups we did confirm should not wait to hear about Jesus while we spent our time and resources looking for unconfirmed groups. More survey work was certainly warranted, but we also wanted to move quickly to begin the disciple-making process among the first set of confirmed groups we had prioritized.

The task of introducing the good news of Jesus to these tribes was now at hand, and people were praying.

THE BIT

Years before the Final 58 project was conceived, Samuel Hatt attended a missions conference in the Midwest of the US. As a missions enthusiast, Samuel had been to many missionary conferences over the years and had become aware of the wide spectrum of ministries in which various organizations were involved—all the way from potable water projects to Bible institutes, from anti-trafficking to evangelism, to Business as Missions and Bible translation. Additionally, numerous organizations highlighted remaining unreached people groups in the world by publishing lists of their names, populations, and countries.

Samuel had a heart for the unreached. He did not have money to support missionaries going to any of them, nor did he feel called to go himself, but he decided that he could pray. *But how to choose from so many?* In the mid-1990s,

Joshua Project had published their list of 1,739 unreached people groups to provide a priority target to reach by the year 2000. In the new millennium, the population threshold for these lists was lowered such that the number grew to well over 7,000 remaining unreached groups.

Samuel wanted to choose a group he was sure others would overlook. Certainly, large groups in well-known nations would be the first to receive all the attention. Samuel determined to choose a very small tribe in a small, relatively unknown country. He figured not many people would pray for them. He chose the Bit of Laos and began lifting them up in prayer. In fact, Samuel was faithful to pray for the Bit daily for at least five years without ever receiving any news about them. Each day he asked God to send them someone who could share the good news message of Jesus.

The entire Bit tribe of Laos only number around 2,000 people. They are located in a remote region of Phongsali province—the northernmost province in Laos. Like most rural tribes, they farm the steep mountainsides and live in villages of wood and thatch houses. They worship the spirits and placate them with sacrifices of chickens and other small animals. Our workers discovered the Bit during the survey phase of the work, and we decided to prioritize them for outreach from the beginning.

A team of three young Lao national missionaries, Vaan, Nok and Boonmi (two women and one man) approached three Bit villages we had mapped out. The process was simple—walk through the village and pray, look for someone with whom they could strike up a conversation, seek ways to bless, and share the gospel of Jesus as the Holy Spirit led. In this way, the teams hoped to locate a person of peace—someone who God prepared to welcome envoys of his message into the village and who could use his or her influence to introduce this message to others.

Vaan, Nok and Boonmi prayer walked faithfully through the first two villages. The reception was cool at best—a few interactions but no real candidates for a person of peace. The team was a bit discouraged, but determined to work the process faithfully, trusting God. Still, nothing. The Bit people our teams encountered did not have any interest in leaving their spirit and ancestor worship behind.

"There is another Bit village further out. Maybe we should try it?" The team discussed whether they should embark down the jungle trail at such a late hour. "Let's do it!" they determined in faith. The path wound around mountains through thick jungle and required them to cross multiple streams. At many points, the trail was unclear. Finally, after a three-hour trek, they arrived at the village of Nam Laa, which sat on the edge of a small river.

The team's custom was to approach the village headman first, if possible. On this occasion, they shared the gospel with many families before finding the headman. The headman welcomed them in and was eager to learn the purpose of their visit. With boldness, they shared the story of Jesus with him and his family.

"We have heard of many things, but no one has ever told us what you are now saying," the headman remarked. The headman and his family put their faith in Christ, along with two other men. Vaan, Nok, and Boonmi led them in prayer to receive Christ.

On the same day, as Vaan, Nok, and Boonmi were trekking through the jungle toward Nam Laa village, another team was visiting a different Bit village, hundreds of kilometers away. Tawee and Lat had visited this village on a previous trip and had found a family that had expressed much interest in the gospel but stopped short of making a decision. Tawee and Lat wanted to follow up with this family and encourage them to follow Christ. They hoped they had not lost the opportunity.

Upon arriving in the village, they feared they had wasted their time. The entire village was celebrating a festival. In Laos, this means a lot of drinking and eating. While drunkenness can make people quite friendly, it is not conducive for reasonable conversation. Tawee and Lat ate well but did not have any opportunity to share the message of Jesus. Feeling as if any effort would be futile until morning, Lat decided to hit the sack for the night.

Tawee, however, stayed up and waited to see what would develop. Finally, a Bit woman approached him. She was seventy-two years old and the matriarch of the family. "Tell me more about what you shared earlier," she requested. Tawee gladly obliged and explained the story of Jesus another time. As she listened, she was stirred to believe. "What must I do?" she asked Tawee, much like the people in Jerusalem had asked the apostle Peter in Acts 2 when they were convicted by his words. Tawee told her about receiving Christ and being baptized into his name.

The Bit matriarch was ready and did not want to wait until morning. Tawee ran to wake Lat and ask for his assistance. In spite of the late hour, complete darkness, and crisp air during that time of year in the north, the old woman made her way down to the river's edge along with Tawee and Lat. There in the dark, with frigid water rushing around them, the first Bit believer was baptized! The moment was caught on a grainy cell phone video by Lat. A simple, yet beautiful, new birth among the Bit people.

The following morning Tawee and Lat rose early to discover the matriarch's family was both sober and interested in learning about this new faith their grandmother had accepted. They listened to her testimony and the message of Jesus. Afterward, they also believed and were baptized. In their joy, they took Tawee and Lat throughout the village to visit all their relatives so that they could share the good news message with them too. In this way, the gospel of Jesus first came to the Bit people.

Soon after these events, I shared the news of the budding Bit church with a private prayer group. Samuel Hatt was a part of this group and was amazed to learn that the Bit were coming to the Lord. He told me how he had been praying for the Bit daily for years and now was excited to hear that God had answered. I was thrilled to learn that Samuel had been praying for so long and amazed at how news of this random people group reached the very man who had chosen to pray for them years before, from a list of more than seven thousand unreached people groups.

THE MUJI

For years, when a Lao government official or other outsider met a person from the Muji tribe, they assumed they were just Akha. Indeed, the three thousand or so Muji people who live in twelve villages in northern Laos belong to the Akha parent group—a large conglomeration of Sino-Tibetan peoples. However, the Muji language and culture are distinct enough that they consider themselves unique. While some Akha-grouped tribes have been reached with the gospel message, many have not. The Muji had never heard about Jesus before the Final 58 project began.

One Muji village Janpeng is buried deep in the jungle-covered mountains of Phongsali and only accessible by motor vehicle in the dry season. During the summer monsoons, visitors must navigate the narrow path leading to the village by foot. In spite of its remote location, Choy and Sone, Lao national missionaries, felt certain the Holy Spirit was leading them to go find a person of Peace ready to receive the gospel. Choy and Sone located the village headman's house as soon as they arrived and began conversing with him and his family. Summarizing the Biblical narrative, they struck a chord when they mentioned Noah and the flood. Like many tribes around the world, the Muji had also heard the story of the great flood from their ancestors. This connection opened up the Muji headman and his brother to listen to more of the gospel story and learn about Jesus. They became very interested.

In spite of the interest, Choy and Sone struggled to share the message of Jesus with the Muji villagers since most of them could not speak Lao. The two men persisted, however, and shared what they could with any Muji Lao speaker they could find. As it turned out, the village headman's brother, Seng, was one of the few who could understand Lao. So, in the evening they returned to Seng's house to spend the night.

Coincidentally, Seng's mother was ailing and partially paralyzed on one side of her body. She could barely move her arm and leg, and she was mostly blind in the eye on the paralyzed side. Choy and Sone had been trained to look for opportunities to bless people—to pray and ask for God's blessing and miraculous healing. Seng's debilitated mother seemed to present the perfect opportunity. Neither Choy nor Sone claimed to possess the gift of healing, but they knew they could ask for anything in prayer if they prayed in faith. With permission, they laid their hands on Seng's mother and began appealing to God for mercy in the name of Jesus. Suddenly, the woman was able to move her arm and leg. Her eye cleared up, and her vision was not as fuzzy as it had been before. The display of God's power convinced her and her friend to put their faith in Jesus.

Before the night was over, word got out in the village about the healing. The villagers began to arrive at the house where Choy and Sone were staying, begging them to pray for numerous ailments. Choy and Sone were overwhelmed and quickly sent a text message to the sending base requesting prayer. In a matter of hours, we received the news and asked groups of prayer partners in the US to pray for the Muji and for Choy and Sone.

Seng, who was also the second village headman, was happy to see his mother healed. He welcomed Choy and Sone to return to the village at any time they pleased. God was opening a door for the national missionaries, and they wanted to make the most of the opportunity to share the good news with the Muji. The next morning, before departing, they met another man named

Kaew. Choy and Sone shared the story of Christ with him, and Kaew likewise put his faith in Jesus!

Two weeks later Choy and Sone made good on Seng's invitation and returned to Janpeng village. Before entering the village, they paused to pray for God's guidance and blessing, as was their custom. After praying, they immediately proceeded to visit Seng's mother and were overjoyed to find her praying to Jesus. They presented a Bible to the family.

That morning Seng's entire household was preparing to head out for a day of work in the upland fields, so Choy and Sone decided it would be good to join in and help them. The walk to the field took more than an hour. As they walked together and worked throughout the day, Choy and Sone took the opportunity to share more about the gospel. The farmers burned some of their field that day, which gave Choy and Sone the opportunity to speak about hell. This topic piqued the family's interest. Another topic of discussion were the ancestral spirits—spirits of deceased parents and grandparents. Each household maintains a shelf-like alter where daily offerings are made to feed the spirits of their ancestors.

According to the Muji custom, any person who touches a spirit altar may be put to death. Choy and Sone asked about this practice. "Why do the spirits of your parents and grandparents forbid you to touch them? Wouldn't you be sad if your children were not allowed to touch you?" The Muji farmers admitted they would. But they could give no better rationale—it was just their custom. In fact, they had never questioned it until Choy and Sone's inquiry started to make them reconsider. "These spirits must not really be the spirits of your beloved parents and grandparents! Rather, they are deceitful spirits only pretending to be them."

Seng contemplated all of these new viewpoints throughout the day. Before they retired that night, he was convinced about the message Choy and Sone were sharing. *Jesus must be the way!* While Choy and Sone baptized the mother and her friend who had believed on their previous visit, Seng and his nephew put their faith in Christ. The following day, Seng conducted a ceremony to remove all the family's spirit paraphernalia from their house and incinerate it.

As the ancestral spirit shelves, strings, and other items went up in smoke, Sai, the third village headman, approached. He invited Seng, Choy, and Sone to visit his house to pray for another ill woman. The three were happy to oblige and hurried to pray for her. Before they finished, Sai also prayed, asking God to heal the woman, even though he had not yet put his faith in Christ!

Before Choy and Sone departed from Janpeng, they learned of yet another man who wanted to believe. Instead of doing it themselves, they instructed Seng to lead him to faith and trained him how to do it.

In the following weeks, many Muji people turned to the Lord, and our team planted the first Muji church in Janpeng village. As a good sign of their sincerity, they gathered their articles of spirit worship, took them out from their houses, and burned them.

New believers do not perform these actions lightly but risk causing a stir in the community and possibly among the authorities. When such drastic steps are taken, two things could potentially happen—it could spark a movement of Muji people turning to Christ as they all begin to see the power of God, or it could ignite a backlash of persecution.

In a place where community decisions trump individual ones, most villagers view destroying spirit houses and articles of worship as upsetting the balance of spiritual peace. Any negative event or misfortune that occurs in the following weeks could be interpreted as an angry response of the spirits—even if it befalls someone who did not believe or is unrelated to the decision to turn to Christ. In such circumstances, the community exerts great pressure on the new believers to recant their faith and turn back to the spirits.

Choy and Sone did an excellent job in discipling and equipping the new Muji believers to share their faith, lead others to Christ, and repeat the discipleship process. An important part of this was to translate their simple Creation-to-Christ gospel story into the Muji language. Sai, the third village headman, spoke enough Lao to help them do this, along with the help of a teenage girl. Because the new Christians are participating in reaching their own people, the Muji church is growing strong.

THE PHOUSANG

"Where are the Phousang people?" Daa and Nok wondered. They were praying for the Phousang tribe as they poured over the map of northern Laos. They discovered that the road leading to the Phousang village of Chitong was narrow and difficult. However, Daa and Nok had faith that this is where God had called them to go and that the Phousang were the tribe God had chosen for them to share the good news message of Jesus.

Daa and Nok represented one of our first two all-female teams of national missionaries. We have been delighted to partner with these faithful young ladies, both single and married, who bear even more risks traveling into the countryside than the men. Yet, God continues to use them mightily.

"God, can you please prepare this tribe to receive Jesus?" Nok prayed fervently. She and Daa wanted to see this tribe reached. The sincerity of their hearts for this people was demonstrated by the passion of their prayers. Such sincerity is a testament to our national missionary partners' authentic faith and desire to serve the Lord. In Lao society concern for those outside of one's own family is rare, and concern for members of a completely different tribe even rarer. It was clear that God had given his concern for the Phousang to Daa and Nok.

Their first trip to the Phousang took them to a remote district in the northernmost province of Laos. This entire region was without electricity and running water. When they arrived in Chitong village, they presented themselves to the village headman before proceeding to engage the villagers. He asked them, "Where did you come from? Why are you here?" They answered as they had been trained. He was kind, if not overtly hospitable, but offered them a place to stay for the night.

Word got out in the village that two young Lao women were spending the night. After dinner, a horde of people visited the village headman's house wanting to meet the strange visitors. They peppered Daa and Nok with questions, "Where did you come from? What tribe are you? What did you come to do?" Daa and Nok patiently answered their questions hoping to satisfy their curiosity. "We came to sell these useful items we brought from the city."

Over the years we have used multiple, and legitimate, platforms for getting our people out into unreached villages—agriculture, pigs, water testing, government survey work, relief projects, and even selling Amway-type products. Each of these have had their advantages and disadvantages. However, we have found that one of the best ways to give Lao people a good reason to frequent outlying villages is to simply load them up with useful things from the city market—rice baskets, knives, soap, shampoo, plastic dishes, tools, clothing, etc.—and sell them to people who rarely have the opportunity to visit the city. The biggest disadvantage with more complicated projects is that the efforts (such as agriculture) can easily be traced to the sending entity, and it becomes a security risk. Selling trinkets, however, is a simple and independent business activity in which many Lao entrepreneurs engage. The biggest advantage with this approach is that there are no obvious connections to the mobilization team. Daa and Nok were equipped as such.

The next morning Daa and Nok did what they promised. They roamed from household to household showing the people their wares. As they did, they also had the opportunity to share about God. But as they told people about Jesus, no one was interested in believing. Not one person came to Christ. Finally, they approached a house of a married couple in their 50s. The husband, Somvang, had been afflicted with an evil spirit for three years. "Only God can save you from the grip of Satan," they told him. He was interested and allowed them to lay their hands on him and pray.

After praying for Somvang, Daa and Nok invited them to hear more. "Do you want to listen to God's story?" Somvang was enthusiastic. "Yes, I want to hear it!" So, they shared the simple Creation-to-Christ gospel story about how God created the world and all people. When they finished, they asked him, "Do you believe this story? Do you want to receive faith?" Somvang answered, "Yes, I want to believe!" Daa and Nok were thrilled finally to witness the miracle of the first Phousang person coming to know Jesus. They prayed with him to receive Christ.

Next, Daa and Nok turned to his wife, "Do you want to put your faith in Jesus too?" But she was not ready. Daa and Nok stayed with Somvang's family and continued to teach them both.

A couple weeks later Daa and Nok made their second trip to Chitong village. They immediately checked in on Somvang. "How is he feeling?" they inquired of his family, wanting to know if the evil spirits had returned to torment him. "He is completely healed!" they replied. Daa and Nok could not stop smiling and gave glory to God. Before Somvang, they had never witnessed God heal someone for whom they prayed. "This is an awesome thing that God has done!" they remarked to each other.

Daa and Nok spent time teaching Somvang about what it means to follow Jesus. They shared scriptures with him and taught the importance of baptism. Daa and Nok did not want to baptize Somvang unless he understood that he could not continue to worship both the spirts and follow Jesus too. He had countless strings tied around his wrist from innumerable animistic ceremonies performed in an attempt to protect him from the evil spirits.

"Do you want to be baptized?" the women asked him. "Yes, I want to be baptized and follow Jesus," Somvang replied. So Daa and Nok took a knife and cut all the strings from his wrists, threw them into the fire, and led him down to the stream to be baptized.

Witnessing her husband's decision, Somvang's wife also became convinced. She had seen how Somvang had changed and asked them if she could follow Christ too. Daa and Nok shared God's story with her, and after praying to receive Jesus, she was baptized into Christ. Then, their 19-year-old son made the same decision and was baptized too. In this way, the good news of Jesus first came to the Phousang.

Nok shared this testimony:

After the baptisms, we had the chance to stay with them and grow close to them. We saw how God did miracles and how the love of Jesus came into their lives. They loved Jesus, and they loved us too. They looked at us as if we were their own children, and we were filled with joy. We praised God for this family and for what God did next too!

Relatives of Somvang and his wife lived next door. They observed what was happening, and then the husband and wife believed, along with their father. Daa and Nok taught this family, too, and baptized them. Two families and six new baptized believers made up the first Phousang church. "I praise God for everything he did in Chitong village!" Nok rejoiced.

Many of our Lao national missionary partners share the gospel in multiple villages of the same people group and occasionally share the good news of Jesus with more than one tribe. Daa and Nok were also making efforts to reach the Phousang village of Namani.

The road to Namani was especially rough, and the young women trudged through deep mud created by torrential rains. They prayed as they entered the village that God would prepare someone to host them. They proceeded to the village headman's house, but he refused to receive them. "I don't know you," he rebuffed. "You are strangers and not one of us!"

Daa and Nok forced a polite smile and continued on their way through the village. They found the second (vice) village headmen, who was hesitant to receive them, too, but did so reluctantly. It was getting dark, and the young women had nowhere else to go. Once inside of his house, his curiosity got the best of him. "What are you doing here? Why, as young women, have you traveled so far to reach our village?" Daa and Nok answered him as best they could. "We have come to sell our wares," they answered but undoubtedly did not satisfy his curiosity. He continued to ask them more questions into the night.

The next morning Daa and Nok went out into the village to sell their items from the market. The people were afraid of them, however, and refused to buy anything. Their attempts were complicated by the fact that most of the Phousang could not speak any Lao language. Again, Daa and Nok did not let this deter them. Instead, they decided to learn the Phousang language.

They only found two or three people in the village who could speak a little Lao. So, Daa and Nok quizzed them on how to say numerous Phousang phrases and dedicated themselves to learn to speak an unknown second language as many a pioneer missionary has done through the ages. Their efforts proved to be the key to unlocking the door to the Phousang people in Namani village. The fact that these Lao women would care enough about them to learn their language afforded them the opportunity to build relationships with the Phousang people.

The following week, when Daa and Nok were set to return to Namani, they remembered the initial cold reception they had received from the villagers. The memory discouraged them as they planned their return. So Daa and Nok prayed, "God, if this is your plan—if you want the Phousang to know you— please open their minds and hearts to see your mercy and goodness! Please cause them to receive us too."

Prayer, persistence, and language study made the difference. When they arrived in Namani, the people readily bought their wares. When they visited people, they were received into their homes. When they saw a sick person, they asked to pray for them, and each time the Phousang villagers allowed the women to pray for healing in Jesus's name. However, the Phousang still were not interested in hearing the story about God. Daa and Nok attempted to share it with a number of people, but they did not understand because of the language barrier.

Finally, Daa and Nok met a married couple in their thirties with whom they shared the simple gospel story about how God created the world and all people. They began cultivating interest with questions. "Do you know where humans originated from? Where did the forests come from? Why are we here on earth?" And they asked many more "why" questions. To all of these, the man answered the same: "I don't know!" It was not something he had ever taken time to consider.

The women continued, "Do you believe in the spirits in your house?" The man answered, "That's right! We worship the spirits." So, they asked him, "Do you know where the spirits come from?" He admitted, "I do not know!" Daa and Nok continued to pique his interest with their questions. "Do you want to know where the trees, people, and spirits come from?" The man and his wife were now very interested. "Yes, please tell us!"

Daa and Nok were just about to begin sharing the Creation-to-Christ gospel story when three more people arrived. They shared the story of how God created the world and everything in it with the entire group. The people listened intently. When Daa and Nok finished, they asked the five of them, "Do you want to believe in Jesus and in the God who created the heavens and the earth? Do you want to have a new life?"

"Oh! Your God is good!" the Phousang villagers replied. "He knows everything!" They were ready to believe. "What must we do to become followers of Jesus?" Daa and Nok answered, "It's not difficult. Repeat our words as we pray." One by one, Daa and Nok led each of them in prayer to receive Jesus. Afterward, they spent time teaching them about life in Christ. They had not taught for even five minutes when four more people showed up, asking, "What are you talking about?" They wanted to see what was happening.

"We are talking about the One who created people and created the world. He is the Almighty God!" The newcomers were also interested. The women asked them, "Do you want to hear this story too?" They answered, "Yes, we want to hear it!" Daa and Nok started from the beginning and shared the entire Biblical narrative with the group of nine people. Now they wanted to place their faith in Jesus too. Daa and Nok led each of them in prayer as they had with the first five.

When they had finished praying, Daa and Nok took the opportunity to begin worship together with the new group of Phousang believers. They took a simple Lao worship song (*Thank you, thank you, God!*) and translated it into the Phousang language. Daa and Nok taught this to the Phousang believers and were excited when they were able to start worshiping God in their own tongue on the first day of their new faith. Everyone was excited, and Daa and Nok saw how God had poured out joy and peace upon these people. The worship continued late into the day, and the women spent the night at the new believers' house.

A deep peace overcame Daa and Nok as they laid down to sleep. "Oh, God is great!" they exclaimed to each other. "Now God has chosen the Phousang tribe to be his children!" Daa and Nok felt that their prayers were being answered for the Phousang people. In spite of initial discouragement and rejection, God had now opened the door of salvation to this remote tribe. Their persistence and prayers had paid off!

MANY MORE TRIBES

By the end of our first full year of engagement, the Final 58 effort in Laos grew dramatically. Twenty-two previously unengaged unreached people groups in Laos now had believers. These were the Yoy, Thai Angkham, Siluh, Laomai, Bit, Samtao, Trui, Phoua, Ngouan, Salang, Akha Kor, Phousang, Muji, Mouteun, Kher, Noowur, Jawhoi, Laoseng, Laopan, Sida, Wueyeu, and Khua tribes. Fifteen new churches had been planted in ten of these tribes, with the beginnings of more in others. Initially, we sent out teams of national missionaries from a northern sending base. Later, we launched a second sending base in the south. Likewise, a new Boot Camp training program began in the south to equip national missionaries there. The total number of national missionaries we mobilized grew from eight to fifty, comprising fifteen teams. Over 260 people expressed first-time faith in Christ and fifty-nine of them followed through with baptism.

Every week I continued to ask our Prayer Force team in the US to pray for all the tribes our teams were engaging. They were faithful to do so, and their "batting average" was almost 1.000. I can't remember any specific prayer request I presented to them that wasn't answered in the way we were asking. However, a common prayer was that the Lord would grow the new believers, multiply the new churches, help them to stand strong in faith, and establish his kingdom. These prayer requests are ongoing.

The vision to see all the tribes in Laos reached with the gospel was well underway. However, we learned quickly that we cannot expect to see progress without opposition.

An enemy prowls around like a lion, looking for someone to devour.

10

OPPOSITION

DAA AND NOK

"If you just sleep with the police chief, we'll let you go!"

Daa and Nok were now in a Phongku village. The Phongku are another unreached tribe living in a remote area in the mountains of northern Laos. Daa and Nok were making trips to share the good news of God's grace to the Phongku as well as the Phousang. None of the Phongku knew about or believed in Jesus. They were a perfect example of a completely unreached tribe in Laos, hidden under the over-arching umbrella of peoples called the Phounoy.

Phounoy in Lao literally means "little people." Like the Akha, many related tribes are lumped together as Phounoy without regard to their cultural and linguistic distinctions. The Phongku are one of these tribes and consist of less than half a dozen villages tucked away in the mountains in two districts.

It was a typical morning in the countryside. Daa and Nok awoke to roosters crowing and the bustle of a mountain village at sunrise. The young women had traveled there the day before and looked forward to seeing who God would lead them to that morning. They prayed together and sauntered through the village peddling their items from the city market. As they did, they looked for opportunities to share the gospel and hopefully meet someone God had prepared as a person of peace to welcome the message into the Phongku tribe.

In remote tribal villages, outsiders are conspicuous. In the same way all of the villagers noticed Daa and Nok's presence, the women noticed the arrival of several police officers to the Phongku village. Daa and Nok were not sure of their purpose but took it as a sign they should depart, avoid any potential problems, and return another day.

They traveled to the next village down the road, which belonged to the Muji people—an Akha-related tribe. Daa and Nok knew this group was also unreached, so they began the same process of selling their wares and looking for a person of peace. *Perhaps God has plans for us in this village today, and so led us here,* they thought. They met a man named Tuan and began to share with him. *Could he be the one?*

Without warning, several police officers on motorcycles sped into the village and surrounded the women. Daa and Nok had no opportunity to avoid them now. The officers jumped off their bikes, grabbed their things, and demanded to know what they were doing. One of the officers discovered a notebook among their possessions and began a frantic search of each page. On one page, he found the word "Jesus" written in Lao, and that was all the evidence they needed.

"Jesus!" they declared, "Do you follow him?"

The women answered boldly, "Yes, we do!"

"Then you must come to the police station with us," the police commanded them.

"No, if you have something to say to us, you can tell us right here, right now." Daa and Nok were trained in how to handle interactions with police, interrogations, and arrest as a part of the Final 58 training program. Consequently, they knew to resist politely and let the police see they were aware of their rights. However, the police officers appeared to be getting more agitated.

"You must come to the station to talk. We have been tracking your movements and activity for the past month, and we're sick and tired of following you all over the place!" they demanded.

Daa and Nok feigned compliance, and in doing so, an opportunity presented itself to escape. This is also a part of their security training. Sometimes escape is a prudent option. In Laos, there are not many effective means for tracking people. Consequently, one can take advantage of this lack of infrastructure and the lethargy of the police investigators to identify their suspects.

In an instant, the women jumped on their motorcycles and attempted to speed away. However, one of the police officers moved more quickly. He grabbed Nok's wrist and clamped it tightly. His grip twisted her arm, and the sharp pain prevented their ability to flee.

Now in police custody, they loaded Daa and Nok's motorbike onto the trailer of a rice-paddy tractor and escorted the women to the nearest police substation in town. The derelict building was not much of a station. Crumbling plaster covered the lower-level walls, and a makeshift jail of particleboard was constructed on top. Because previous detainees had nowhere to relieve themselves, the room reeked with the stench of urine. The police forced the women into this upper room and locked the door.

For some reason, the police had not yet confiscated Daa and Nok's cell phones. Once in the privacy of the jail room, they took the opportunity to delete all potentially incriminating information—pictures, text messages, and social media apps. Nok removed the SIM card from her phone and successfully discarded it. Then they waited and prayed.

Daa and Nok had not eaten since early that morning, before being arrested, and it had only been a small breakfast. They were not sure if the police would provide food to them or not, but they knew the police would never pay for anything. They entreated the guard with a request to eat and eventually were allowed to leave under police escort. They purchased some food at a nearby store with their own money.

Later that afternoon, the police began their official interrogation of Daa and Nok. They searched their belongings, laid out all their notebooks, and page by page took pictures of everything written in them. They took their time to sit them down, act as stern and serious as possible, and began to ask them pointed questions.

"Why do you follow Jesus? Why do you believe in this foreign religion?" In Laos, the communist propaganda contends that Christianity is a foreign religion and that those who accept it have betrayed their nation and cultural heritage. Their questions, riddled with reproach, were designed to melt the women's resolve.

Daa and Nok deftly answered all the questions following the security training they had received. This frustrated the police who wanted to see confessions, apologies, and recantations of faith in Christ. They threatened to kill them. "We can execute traitors, you know?"

At one point, Daa boldly declared to the police, "Our God is the great God!" The police responded with anger and attempted to handcuff the two women together as punishment. Daa and Nok resisted. They didn't know if they were about to be killed and if this was their last chance to survive. A struggle ensued, and several police officers chased Daa and Nok around the room, doing their best to subdue them and lock them up while the women did their best to evade restraint. Their vigorous resistance escalated the situation until one of the women lost her cool.

"You're stupid!" she shouted at the man, which was obviously not what she was trained to say. Consequently, it infuriated the police officers who exerted greater force to overpower the women. The police succeeded in restraining them, put on handcuffs, and shoved them into a back room. They locked the door and stationed a guard to watch them. Daa and Nok were shaken, but all they could do was pray and wait to see what would happen. Their lives were in God's hands.

Because of the scuffle, the police had clamped the handcuffs tightly. After a few hours, the cuffs began to cut into the skin on the women's wrists. The pain was agonizing. They knew a plea to the police officers would not result in mercy after their defiant display. Instead, they prayed, "God, please give us relief and please give us the strength to endure whatever happens." Just as they said, "Amen" a police officer came in and removed the handcuffs from their wrists. Without explanation, they separated the two women into different rooms. Tears welled in their eyes as Daa and Nok considered they might never see each other again. Then the police put Nok to work doing the men's laundry.

At one point, Nok noticed a woman walk into the police station who looked familiar. She realized that it was Lena, a classmate of hers from years before when she attended college in the city. She was surprised to see her in this remote district of a completely different province in Laos. "What are you doing here?" Lena asked Nok. Nok told her that she and Daa had been arrested for being Christians and accused of spreading religion. Lena told Nok, "Don't go out preaching anymore!" Lena was concerned for Nok's wellbeing since she understood the animosity the police had toward Christians. As it turned out, Lena was now the wife of the corrupt police officer who had first confiscated Nok's identification card. But Lena proved to be a helpful friend and mercy from God.

The police proceeded to interrogate Daa and Nok at random times throughout the day. They wanted to know who had sent them out to spread religion in the countryside and what kind of system they belonged to. "Who is your boss?" they demanded to know. "How long have you been working for this society?" Daa and Nok replied truthfully that they did not have a boss but that they were just selling items they had purchased themselves. Throughout the entire interrogation, both Daa and Nok did not cower in fear but did an excellent job following the proper protocol for successfully enduring a police interrogation without divulging sensitive information. They deflected questions, repeated simple truthful statements, and did not leave the interrogators anywhere to go.

Being less than satisfied with their unfruitful interrogation, the police continued to demean Daa and Nok. They forced them to act as bar girls and serve whiskey to the police. This lasted until midnight as the police got drunk and carried on. The more they drank, the more obnoxious they became. "Come sleep with the police chief!" they badgered them. "If you just sleep with him, we'll let you go! We promise—we'll give you everything back, and you can go home." The police pressured the women repeatedly.

Daa and Nok steadfastly refused. But they were not off the hook. As punishment, the police put them back into the ramshackle latrine cell to spend the night. The room was dark, moist, and full of garbage, insects, and mosquitos. The stench of urine caused them to gag once more. The women begged for a broom to sweep up the mess and clear a place to sleep and were finally given one. At this time, Lena brought Daa and Nok a blanket and pillow to share, along with a mat to cover the floor. They spent the rest of the night in this dirty room, but sleep was sparse.

During the night, Daa and Nok prayed and meditated on scripture. They didn't know at what point one of the men might come in, pull them out, or force himself upon them. Nok was comforted by the words of Psalm 23, which she had memorized:

You, LORD, are my shepherd. I will never be in need. You let me rest in fields of green grass. You lead me to streams of peaceful water, and you refresh my life. You are true to your name, and you lead me along the right paths. I may walk through valleys as dark as death, but I won't be afraid. You are with me, and your shepherd's rod makes me feel safe. You treat me to a feast, while my enemies watch. You honor me as your guest, and you fill my cup until it overflows. Your kindness and love will always be with me each day of my life, and I will live forever in your house, LORD. (Psalm 23:1-6 CEV)

Daa thought of other scriptures that spoke about persecution, including the words of Jesus in Matthew 5:

God blesses those people who are treated badly for doing right. They belong to the kingdom of heaven. God will bless you when people insult you, mistreat you, and tell all kinds of evil lies about you because of me. Be happy and excited! You will have a great reward in heaven. People did these same things to the prophets who lived long ago. (Matthew 5:10-12 CEV)

God kept them safe through the night.

When the police convened the following morning, a discussion ensued about what to do with the women. Some thought they should take them to the main district police station and escalate the issue. This would have meant a longer sentence and more time in jail. However, it might also expose the mistreatment of the women by the corrupt police substation officers. In the end, they decided to escort Daa and Nok to the main road and drop them there. Nok's friend Lena was able to contact our sending base to keep us posted about the police's discussion. Lena revealed that her husband intended to keep their bags, possessions, and motorcycle.

In the afternoon, two police officers drove motorcycles with Daa and Nok riding on the back of each. One of the motorcycles belonged to the women. Daa and Nok didn't want to go with them, but they were not given a choice in the matter. They took them out to the main road. As they drove, they purposely swerved and turned in order to scare Daa and Nok. They spoke rudely and openly mocked the young women. The man escorting Nok kept trying to fondle and grab her inappropriately as they drove.

The two officers promised that once they reached the main road, they would return the women's motorcycle and effects so they could proceed home. However, it was only a ruse to get them to comply. Once they arrived, they dumped the women off and sped away with both motorcycles, stranding them on the side of the road before they could do anything to stop them. Daa and Nok had their phones and called the substation chief to complain. This proved unfruitful, however. The chief just yelled at the women and blamed them. He claimed they could get their motorcycle back in five days, but Daa and Nok knew it had been stolen.

Still, Daa and Nok refused to go away quietly. In line with their training, they threatened the police chief with further action in the higher courts. The treatment of the women by the police was unlawful, immoral, and unacceptable. However, the chief continued to blame Daa and Nok—"It is your fault because you follow Jesus!"

So Daa and Nok started walking. They did not have a motorcycle, and there was no bus. It would take days to walk all the way home, which was in a different province. But God provided a passing truck to give them a ride to the next town. They waited there until Nok's fiancé came to retrieve them. Daa and Nok arrived back at the sending base around 8:30 p.m., shaken, but standing firm.

After a period of rest and debriefing, Daa and Nok continued their mission work and headed back out to remote villages sharing the good news of Jesus with the unreached.

JESUS'S FOOD

A while later I had the opportunity to encourage all of our national missionary teams at the sending base. As I prayed about what to share, the Lord put Daa and Nok's story on my heart, as well as other trials our Lao brothers and sisters were facing because of the gospel.

In the fourth chapter of the gospel of John, Jesus famously talks to the woman at the well. She was a Samaritan, and as a result, a hidden unreached people group in the eyes of the Jews. Jesus was very interested in their salvation, but the disciples were completely unaware of the spiritual breakthrough that was happening. When they returned to find Jesus talking to a Samaritan woman, they were surprised. Perhaps they thought it was inappropriate on both counts—her being a Samaritan and a woman. They attempted to turn Jesus's attention to the food they had just purchased, and he replied, "I have food to eat that you know nothing about" (John 4:32 NIV). The disciples were confused, still not understanding what was motivating Jesus. Jesus explained, "My food is to do the will of him who sent me and to finish his work" (John 4:34 NIV). Jesus told his disciples to "open your eyes and look at the fields! They are ripe for harvest" (John 4:35 NIV).

Jesus wanted his disciples to be on the same page as him. They were on a completely different page. Their purpose was to eat lunch. Jesus's purpose was to reap a spiritual harvest—to bring salvation to many unreached Samaritans. Jesus cared so much about this that he would rather share the gospel than eat.

When we have the eyes of Jesus and when we hunger for the food of doing his will and completing his task, we can endure anything—even going without food. Our physical needs become secondary to our primary purpose of leading people out of darkness and sin and into God's great mercy and forgiveness.

I shared the message about Jesus's food with our team of national missionaries. I also shared with them how the apostle Paul hungered for this food more than any other. Paul was on the same page with Jesus and endured all manner of suffering for the sake of offering the message of salvation to those who had never heard it before. In 2 Corinthians 11 Paul talked about how he had worked so hard, been severely flogged, exposed to death multiple times, been whipped, beaten and pelted with stones, was shipwrecked and spent a night and day in the open sea, and gone without food and clothing—all to do the will of the one who sent him. That will was to open the eyes of the unreached Gentiles so that they would turn from darkness to light, be released from the power of Satan to the power of God, and receive forgiveness of sins and reconciliation with God (Acts 26:18). When we are on mission and when we have eyes for the kingdom of God, we can endure all the opposition before us. But if we do not really believe in what we are doing, we will choose an easier path.

Both Jesus and Paul had eyes for the kingdom of God, and both endured much physical suffering to see that kingdom born into the world.

The message was quite fitting. The following week all the Lao national missionary teams would face persecution like never before. Several were detained and interrogated by the police. All four of the women experienced attempted sexual assault while in the village. Another team had to spend the night alone in the jungle since the village they were visiting refused to accept them. After being detained and questioned by the police, one of the young men abandoned his teammate in the field and returned home.

One team, Pawn and Souk, had their first experience with arrest and interrogation.

PAWN AND SOUK

Pawn and Souk traveled all morning until they reached a Khmu village. They stopped there to rest and decided to take the opportunity to share the gospel. One family who seemed receptive took them in and listened to the message they were sharing. The family fed them a late lunch and encouraged Pawn and Souk to rest, since they had been traveling for the bulk of the day. Pawn and Souk thanked them for their hospitality and hit the sack. They napped until 4 p.m. that evening.

Something changed while Pawn and Souk slept. The family who received them grew suspicious and feared they may be hosting outlaws. They called and reported Pawn and Souk to the police. Because it was already late, however, the police did not respond. Pawn and Souk made plans to spend the night, but the family would not allow them to stay any longer. After searching, they could not find anyone else in the village to receive them either. Pawn and Souk departed while it was late and wound up spending the night in an abandoned roadside hut.

The following morning, as Pawn and Souk were traveling down the road, three police motorcycles swept in behind them, and a police pickup truck swooped in front of them, blocking their way. The police demanded that Pawn and Souk get into the truck and return to the police station with them. Pawn and Souk refused, insisting that the police talk to them there in the middle of the road. "There's no need to go to the police station in town when we can talk right here." But the police gave them no choice. They forced Pawn and Souk into the pickup. Souk's heart began beating wildly from that point and all the way to the police station. They prayed that God would help them.

When they walked into the interrogation room at the police station, Pawn and Souk were overcome with an unexplainable sense of peace. All their fear departed, and they stopped shaking. The police questioned them, and they gave the right answers repeatedly, as they had been trained. Four police officers stood over and behind Souk while one of them pulled out a knife to threaten him. But Souk did not waver. Sensing that the young men were not as intimidated as they should be, one of the police officers became enraged. He struck Souk in the eye with his fist, knocking him from his chair. In the fall, Souk injured his back. But in spite of this maltreatment, Pawn and Souk continued to be filled with peace and a complete absence of fear.

In fact, during the interrogation, God filled Pawn and Souk with laughter. They did not understand why they felt like laughing. Pawn and Souk had never experienced this before. They did their best to hold it in during the interrogation out of respect for the interrogators, who were infuriated that they could not obtain any information from the young men.

In the end, the police escorted Pawn and Souk to the bus station, purchased tickets with the team's money, and sent them packing back to the sending base city. Before the police released them, Pawn overheard one of the police officers talking on the phone to another officer at the destination. "When they arrive there, if they stay together, arrest them!"

Several hours later Pawn and Souk arrived home, and as they disembarked, they noticed two police officers coming their way. So, they split up, lost anyone who may have been tailing them, and reconvened at the sending base.

Pawn and Souk were all smiles when they finally greeted the others on the Final 58 team. From the time they were arrested, they had not had anything to eat or drink. The others took them out for a meal of fried noodles, which they wolfed down. As they ate, they excitedly shared their experience with the rest of the team. Pawn and Souk felt like they had come through the experience victoriously and that their faith grew as a result. Now they were grateful to be back.

Pawn and Souk were the first of our Lao national missionaries to be physically beaten by the authorities. They would not be the last.

JAI AND BOON

By early 2020, we had nearly ten classes of boot campers who had finished their training and progressed to being mobilized as national missionaries. Before they can graduate from Boot Camp all of them must complete their Faith Journey. Existing national missionaries pray for them as they depart on these excursions, and the boot campers pray for the national missionaries each week as they go out to the field. Seeing the national missionaries come and go each week is an encouragement for boot campers who are being trained to do the same. Having good examples of those who have gone before them, completed their own Faith Journeys, and successfully reached unreached peoples is one of the best ways to raise up new generations of Lao national missionaries.

Just as boot campers on their Faith Journeys have real opportunities to share the gospel and lead people to Christ, they are also exposed to arrest and persecution. Jai and Boon, two new recruits in their 30s, experienced this firsthand on their Faith Journey to Bokeo province.

With limited use of cell phones during the Faith Journey, communication with the teams can be difficult. Usually we do not hear from them until the five days are complete and they arrive back at the meeting point. The time for rendezvous came and went, but there was still no sign of Jai and Boon. We began to hear whispers from contacts in the region that they had been arrested.

After more investigation, we learned that Jai and Boon were indeed in jail under the pretext of being Chinese spies. The police apprehended them on the second day of their journey after they shared the gospel with numerous people and witnessed one man miraculously healed. Somehow, a few local Christians learned about Jai and Boon and brought food to them in jail. Since prisons in Laos do not provide adequate sustenance, families of those incarcerated are responsible for delivering meals to the prison guards each day. The Christians in Bokeo graciously took this charity upon themselves.

We also heard reports that Jai had divulged to the police details about the Final 58 effort and shared real names of both Lao and expatriate partners with them. We were alarmed but asked for all of our supporters around the world to pray. We did not yet have all the facts and did not want to jump to any conclusions. When our team finally made contact with the local authorities, the police leveraged all they learned about the effort in an attempt to extort payment for Jai and Boon's release. When the team didn't budge, the police threatened to send the case to court, where it would be bogged down for months and result in maximum penalty.

After many delays and trips back and forth from the sending base to Bokeo, it appeared that negotiations had failed and the case was going to court. The entire Final 58 team was frustrated and prayed that God would protect us. In the end, it was just another ruse and attempt to extort a bribe. Technically, Laos has freedom of religion in the constitution. However, district police officers commonly take advantage of the public's ignorance of this law. Since people commonly believe that Christianity is an illegal religion, they use this to extort money. In reality, corrupt police officials are occasionally held accountable for using their positions to persecute religious minorities. Escalating the issue to the higher levels may only expose their corruption, so local police are loath to do so, preferring to handle matters in house and pocket any ransoms paid.

In prison, the police separated Jai and Boon and manipulated them through interrogation techniques and torture. The interrogators repeatedly beat them from head to toe, including their privates. They used electric rods to shock them. When they collapsed, they beat them more; when they rose back up, they continued to pummel them with great force.

The jail cell conditions were complete squalor. Human feces covered the floor. Without any proper latrine, prisoners relieved themselves on the ground, retrieved what they could of their excrement, and deposited it into a central tub. The only source of water was a foul-smelling dribble that caused them to vomit. The police put Jai and Boon in stocks and chained their legs to a large immovable block of wood. The immobilization prevented them from relieving themselves on the floor as usual, which forced them to soil themselves. As a result of the chains, Jai's legs swelled extensively.

The police could not produce a confession to being Chinese spies. They finally went after Jai and Boon's faith. Extracting a confession through torture for another crime gives corrupt police a way to claim they are not persecuting Christians for their faith should their arrest ever become public or reach a higher court. Since they didn't succeed, they continued to torture Jai and Boon until they found out all they could about their Christian activity and the Boot Camp training center. A week of torture had passed, and about the time we made contact with the police department regarding Jai and Boon's arrest, they ceased interrogations.

For the second week in prison, Jai and Boon could move about more freely. They said to each other, "They are accusing us of spreading religion, and we have come to announce the kingdom of God. We may as well get on with it!" Jai and Boon surmised that if God led them to jail then that is where he wanted them to shine their light. In spite of their circumstances, Jai and Boon decided to share the good news message with the other prisoners.

Jai and Boon each shared the story of Jesus with ten or so men. A few of the prisoners believed the message, and Jai and Boon even baptized one of them. Under lock and key, there was no way to do a full immersion, as they would normally practice. Consequently, Jai and Boon gathered as much of the foul-smelling water they could and poured it over the repentant man as he made his appeal for inclusion into God's family.

The other men began to respect the faith of Jai and Boon and requested prayer. A two-year drought had ravaged the region so prayer for rain was requested. Even though it was the middle of dry season, a few days later rain fell from the heavens in torrents. Another prisoner asked for prayer that someone would visit him and bring him food. He had not had a visit in the past four to five months. Jai and Boon prayed for him, and a few days later his family came to visit. Moved to tears, which streamed down his face, the man thanked Jai and Boon profusely. Jai and Boon said that all thanks belonged to God and turned the man's attention to the Lord Almighty.

Most importantly, both Jai and Boon held tightly to God's promises in scripture. Their faith overcame the onslaught of lies and hopelessness that would normally attack people who endure such cruel circumstances. When their strength was completely spent, the words of Jesus lifted them up and gave them courage. Instead of merely surviving, Jai and Boon found victory!

After sixteen days in prison, Jai and Boon were released right when we thought the case was being handed over to the judicial system. The COVID-19 virus was already shutting society down, but because the police in Bokeo learned about the Boot Camp operation, the team decided it was necessary to relocate everything to a different urban center in Laos. This was no small task, but the virus lockdown helped to keep the investigation at bay while the transition was made.

YOY PERSEVERANCE

At our southern sending base, one of our boot campers reached out to a Yoy tribal person by cell phone during the COVID-19 lockdown. He shared the good news message of Jesus over the phone, and the first Yoy person received Christ in this way. When things began to open back up, a national missionary team visited this believer and shared the story of Jesus with other villagers in this previously unengaged unreached people group. Soon afterward, our partners baptized the first six Yoy people into Christ.

A few days later, the district police stormed this village when the national missionaries were gone. They arrested all six of the new Yoy believers and brought them to the district police station. They booked them and began the interrogation process. We learned of their arrest and immediately began praying. None of these Yoy believers went through security training and our national missionary team had not yet instructed them on how to endure persecution. We were afraid that they would be pressured to leave the faith and give in to fear.

The police called the parents of each of the new believers. They threatened expulsion from their village and the relinquishing of all their property if anyone persisted in following Jesus. When we learned of this, I immediately sent out a request for prayer for our Yoy brothers and sisters. We asked God to keep them strong and not yield to fear. This was the critical spiritual battle. How they fared in this fight would largely determine how deeply the gospel would take root among the Yoy going forward. Should they bear the brunt of the initial wave of opposition, standing firm, others among them would be able to turn to Jesus much more readily. However, if in the face of threats, they acquiesced to fear and recanted their faith, it would construct a difficult barrier for the gospel in the future. Consequently, hundreds of God's children around the globe went to battle on their knees for the Yoy.

A fellow villager, acting as an informant, reported the new Yoy believers to the police. This was all too typical. Persecution against Christians in Laos usually occurs when jealous neighbors turn them in. In the end, however, the Yoy brothers and sisters remained firm. The police could not do much to them regarding their beliefs since they had not broken any laws. They were released the next day. We were overjoyed when we received the translated report: "All still strong and good faith in Christ."

THE FAITH OF PETER

Battles against persecution do not always end in victory. Victory is not the retention of property, freedom, or even life. On the contrary, when it comes to spiritual battles, victory is the retention of strong faith in Jesus and a heart to pursue him. Sometimes, this battle is lost when young Christians give into their fears. New believers recanting their faith when threatened with persecution is not unheard of. These new believers are as young and vulnerable as you can imagine, and they do not possess the faith of Peter.

Peter, if you remember, was the disciple of Jesus who was the most outspoken. He witnessed a miraculous catch of fish and, as a result, decided to become a fisher of men. He heard Jesus teach, and he watched Jesus heal people. He saw Jesus transfigured before him, and he walked on the surface of the water. Over the course of three years, he was an eyewitness to countless miracles and allowed Jesus to wash his feet. Yet when in fear for his own life, he denied knowing Jesus three times in rapid succession.

The Lord still used Peter. He repented with tears and recommitted to following Jesus. Peter served the Lord boldly from that time forward. Our hope for all our Lao brothers and sisters who give into fear and recant their faith in Christ is that they will be reinstated in the same way Jesus reinstated Peter. But even when our disciples recant or fail to return to faith in Christ, we know we must not be discouraged. We must continue to press on.

When our partners Daa and Nok initially shared the good news of Jesus with the Phousang people high in the mountains, an eighty-year-old grandmother was one of the first to believe in Jesus. She subsequently led a few of her friends to the Lord too. Soon thereafter, some of the village elders struck back.

They threatened police action against the grandmother. She and her friends were frightened, and they turned away from their new faith.

If you would, please pause right now and pray for this grandmother, her friends, and others who have recanted their faith. Pray that the Holy Spirit would continue to work in their hearts to believe and to grow their faith larger than their fears. Pray that they would be reinstated, like Peter, and go on to fruitful kingdom service. Thank you.

A TRAP

In one of the Kher villages, another unreached tribe among whom our partners had planted a church, a team of three female national missionaries—Lana, Vaan and Ella—arrived to encourage the small gathering of believers. Immediately, they noticed that something seemed amiss. The believers they had led to the Lord and had discipled were acting differently. They seemed disturbed. It was strange, but no one explained what was really happening. The young women were confused but proceeded to spend the night with one of the families as usual.

The next morning a group of more than twenty men, led by the village headman, approached the women. He asked them to share the gospel message with them. Lana, Vaan and Ella were cautious but excited about the possibility that so many men, and the village headman, had interest in following Jesus. They gladly accepted the invitation and began sharing.

A few minutes into the story, the police arrived. Then the women realized that the men had set a trap for them. The men had ensnared them by asking them to teach, which allowed the police to catch them in the act. The police told the women to continue and finish their message. Their hearts fluttered at this point, but the women felt that they should make the most of the opportunity and trust the power of the gospel. So, they completed their presentation for everyone, including the police. Afterward, they were taken into custody.

At the police station, the women were insulted, threatened, and interrogated for hours. Under threat of physical violence and to be thrown into the men's prison, all of them unlocked their smart phones for the police. One of the young women had a vast number of pictures, documents, and audio recordings, to which the police gained access. All of these were very incriminating regarding their ministry and the entire Final 58 effort.

That night in jail, Lana, Vaan, and Ella encouraged each other with scripture and prayer. The following day the interrogation continued. The police ordered them to share the gospel message again while ten of them listened and recorded video. With all of the evidence they needed, the police released the three women late in the afternoon, and the team returned home.

It was a worst-case-scenario security breach. The police saved all of this data onto the station computer and used it to pursue a wider investigation into the Final 58 project. Along with the incident with Jai and Boon in Bokeo, these events led to the Final 58 team pulling up stakes in the northern sending base city and completely refining our security training and processes. As a result, national missionaries no longer bring smart phones with them into the field. We relocated the Boot Camp and sending bases, along with most of the expatriate staff. The first four months of the COVID-19 lockdown afforded us the opportunity and cover to reorganize completely.

The Final 58 mission continues in faith. Though we try to be as clever and disciplined as possible, we know that ultimately it is God who keeps things going, not our own strategic savvy. One of our seasoned national missionary partners Choy put it this way: "If it isn't God's timing, then it doesn't matter how much information the police have; they cannot do anything with it."

FRUIT FROM STANDING FIRM

Meanwhile, in the south, one of our national missionary teams reached out to the Makong Pua tribe. God paved a way for the gospel, and they were very fruitful. Our national missionary team led more than thirty people to Christ in one village. Throughout the country, very few villages have had a better response to the gospel. Yet, we never forgot that when people turn to the Lord, there is bound to be a backlash.

It did not take long. Soon after the decisions to follow Christ, Tone, one of the national missionaries on the Makong Pua team, was called into the police station. They were investigating reports of the Makong Pua tribe turning to Christianity. A prayer alert was sent out and many people around the globe began praying for Tone and the Makong Pua people, waiting anxiously to hear news of how the interrogation went.

In a show of solidarity, and by God's grace, the Makong Pua village headman accompanied Tone to the police station. For every question they asked, the village headman assisted Tone in answering. He used his position and influence to bring credibility to all the actions of our national missionary team and the new Makong Pua believers.

The interrogation lasted for more than two hours. When they were finished, Tone had received an incredible result: not only did the police allow the Christians to continue to believe, but they also permitted open worship and continued evangelism! They granted the right to all the Makong Pua villagers to accept Christ freely without any threat of prosecution.

The outcome was beyond what we could ask for or imagine and was the fruit of boldly standing firm in faith! Never before, in the entire country of Laos, have we seen a door for the gospel open as wide as this!

Consequently, the number of Makong Pua believers continued to grow. Just three months later, more than 80 percent of the people in this village had placed their faith in Jesus. Our national missionary partners planted a strong and growing church. Soon, all the surrounding Makong Pua villages also had believers. In fact, the number of believers in this tribe grew so rapidly, they quickly surpassed the threshold of being considered reached.

We praised the Lord for the movement among the Makong Pua people and prayed that in addition to becoming firmly rooted in faith, the Makong Pua would send out their own missionaries to other tribes around them too.

Less than two months later, our prayers were answered. The next cycle of Boot Camp in the south produced fifteen new national missionary recruits. All these recruits came from the tribes our teams had reached during the previous twelve months: Phuthai, Thaiwang, Yoy, Trui, Ta-Oy, Ngouan, and Makong Pua.

Standing firm proved to be fruitful. A second generation of national missionaries was born.

When faced with opposition, the Christ-follower has two basic choices: shrink or stand firm. One way is expedient, the other frightening. One path succumbs to fear, the other faces it. Only in the latter, however, lies the possibility of the extraordinary.

I call this path the Faith Road.

11

THE FAITH ROAD

ELLA

Ella broke down in tears as she spoke. The words would not come out. As she choked up, a hush fell upon the audience of more than fifty fellow national missionaries. The testimony of her first arrest was a sensitive moment recalling the fear and hardship. Her partner, Laa, brought her a tissue, then embraced and stood with her until she finished her testimony.

Ella is a young Khmu woman from Bokeo province. Around the time police arrested Daa and Nok, she joined the Final 58 Boot Camp to be trained to become a national missionary. To complete her training, Ella participated in the Faith Journey as the third member of an all-female team.

Ella and her team traveled by bus to a northern province. They spent the first night in town before heading out to the countryside. Without a vehicle, the women took off from the bus station on foot. They walked for hours and spent the second night in one of the villages along the way, but no one offered them anything to eat. The next day they continued on their way, walking past numerous villages, until they arrived at a Tai Daeng community. Their plan was to find a person of peace, bless the people they met, and look for opportunities to share the gospel. They would not ask for food or lodging, but trust in God and rely upon the hospitality initiated by strangers.

As soon as they arrived, eight policemen carrying assault rifles met them at the entrance to the village. Immediately, they stopped the women and began to investigate them. Since Ella and her team had yet to talk with anyone in the village, she thought to herself, *What did we do wrong?* It did not matter, however, as the police recognized that the women were outsiders. The police demanded their identification cards while they phoned their commanding officer in town.

"I don't have an ID card," Ella informed the men. The other two women produced theirs, but not Ella. The policemen whispered among themselves then turned to the women, "Since she does not have an ID card, you all must stay with us. We will keep you until someone you know can return with documentation to verify your identity."

Ella's hands began to tremble and her eyes widened. She was the only one without an ID card, but she knew her team would never abandon her, even if the police let the other two go. In her heart, she prayed earnestly for God to intervene. He did. The commander refused to retrieve the women and the soldiers had no way to transport them. So, instead of detaining her in the village, they ordered Ella and her team to return to town on foot and appear at the police station there. They wrote up a report and had the women stamp their thumbs in red ink as signatures before releasing them.

As they journeyed back to town, the three women reached one of the first villages they had passed on the way out. All of a sudden, a horde of fifty or more people ran out of the village and surrounded the three young women. Quite agitated, the mob yelled at them and did not allow them to proceed. The village authorities detained them for hours as they wrote up another report, had the women stamp their thumbprints on it in red, and then allowed them to continue to town for yet another interrogation.

It took the rest of the daylight hours to make the return trip. The women still had not eaten anything. Tired and hungry, Ella's feet swelled as each step shot a jolt of pain up her legs. Before reaching town, police in another village they passed detained and interrogated the women and wrote up a third report on them. Once in town, a woman they met allowed them to spend the night.

Early the next morning, Ella and her team reported to the district police office. The officers spent more than seven hours interrogating the women. They separated them into different rooms and deployed six policemen for each girl they questioned, alternating between good cop and bad cop tactics. They tried to extract confessions to crimes of human trafficking or selling drugs. Several times, one of the angry policemen threatened to strike Ella, slapping the table, standing up quickly, and aggressively pointing his finger in her face. He vowed not to let her go until she confessed to the truth.

All three women were famished while they endured the harsh treatment. They had not eaten a full meal for three days. Ella had never experienced a trial like this before. It was a test of her faith to rely upon God and maintain the right attitude. Finally, late in the day, the police decided to release the women. They had no evidence of any crime with which to charge them, and could not elicit a confession. They wrote up a report and had the women mark it with a red thumbprint—the fourth time in two days. Then they ordered the women to march to the local bus station to make their way home.

The police were concerned the women might attempt to return to the village, so they followed them to the bus terminal and notified the station officials to keep an eye on them. Because of the late hour, however, no bus would leave until the following morning. The women resigned themselves to sleeping outside at the station among the stench of trash and under a barrage of biting mosquitoes. In spite of this, they encouraged one another with scripture and held hands to pray for God's help. When the morning light came, Ella and her team caught the bus home.

After a time of rest and debriefing, Ella faced another crisis of faith. A trusted Christian pastor badgered her to give up her role as a national missionary. "Why must you take so many risks to serve God?" he pleaded with her. "How many years will you serve like this?" Ella did not know how to answer him. The pastor said to her, "You are very gifted. You could serve God in an established church! You could teach the children. You do not need to put yourself in so much danger! Quit this outreach now!" Others mocked Ella for serving as a national missionary. "That is work for men! Women should serve in the church. Only stupid women go out to preach the gospel like that!"

The naysaying took its toll on Ella. The words of her friends and pastor began to make sense. She knew they cared for her, and their counsel appeared wise. As she searched her heart, she realized that she had lost her desire to serve as a national missionary. She didn't want to experience the trials as she had before. The recollection of the arrest brought back the tears and trembling. She was void of peace. *Was it necessary to face these great risks in order to serve God? Wouldn't a safer option be just as legitimate?*

Ella thought and prayed about what she would do. Serving God joyfully in the safety of her home village was very appealing. Then, as she prayed, the Lord led her to the following scripture:

If any of you want to be my followers, you must forget about yourself. You must take up your cross and follow me. If you want to save your life, you will destroy it. But if you give up your life for me, you will find it.

(Matthew 16:24-25 CEV)

The Holy Spirit spoke to Ella. She knew that God did not call her to take the easy road, even though she could justify it spiritually. Instead, she decided to hold on to these words of Jesus and fight the good fight. No matter the struggle, she was going to continue in her calling to the unreached tribes of Laos. A smile broke across her face and hope filled her eyes. Suddenly, Ella was filled with courage and strength to persevere. Her joy returned.

The Lord directed Ella to another scripture from the book of Isaiah:

The LORD gives strength to those who are weary. Even young people get tired, then stumble and fall. But those who trust the LORD will find new strength. They will be strong like eagles soaring upward on wings; they will walk and run without getting tired. (Isaiah 40:29-31 CEV)

Finally, Ella was no longer weary or fearful. With a choice of two paths before her, Ella took the road of faith. Trust in Jesus who called her and the promise of God to sustain her, solidified her resolve. She continued her service as a national missionary despite her family's misgivings and her pastor's advice. Ella went on to lead unreached people to the Lord among the Thai Yang and Phousang tribes. She also successfully endured another arrest—the trap set for her, Lana, and Vaan described in the previous chapter. Her faith and testimony have encouraged other national missionaries not to throw in the towel when the going gets tough.

MOVING MOUNTAINS

"But I can promise you this. If you had faith no larger than a mustard seed, you could tell this mountain to move from here to there. And it would. Everything would be possible for you." (Matthew 17:20 CEV).

I was sitting in a Lao house church. The pastor read these words of Jesus and asked the group to discuss their meaning. It wasn't long before participants voiced the two insights I was expecting to hear.

The first was that the mountain Jesus spoke of in this passage was metaphorical. Anxiety, worries and fears in our life are the mountains that our faith can overcome through prayer and meditation.

The second was that God would move the mountain if it was his will.

It may help to look at the context of this scripture. The disciples were trying to heal a boy possessed by an evil spirit. When they couldn't do it, Jesus appeared frustrated and said, "You people are too stubborn to have any faith! How much longer must I be with you? Why do I have to put up with you?" (Matthew 17:17 CEV). Later, when the disciples asked Jesus why they couldn't do it, he did not say, "Because it was not God's will" or "It was not God's time." Instead, he said, "It is because you don't have enough faith!" (Matthew 17:20 CEV). The piece of this puzzle that was lacking was not God's will, but the disciples' faith.

With faith in God, impossible things can happen. Mountains we could never move on our own can be tossed into the sea.

Certainly, we can never treat faith as a toy by which we have the power to do miracles against God's will and according to our own. If we did, we might wield the power like magic to amuse ourselves and others. God's will must be a part of the equation, as our faith in him is not going to accomplish something he does not want. Like the centurion in Luke 7, faith begins when we recognize and acknowledge the realities of the spiritual realm: that all authority belongs to Jesus and the miraculous happens at his command, not just because of our internal effort. Faith is more than holding our spiritual tongue in the right position.

However, neither can we blame God when something we ask for doesn't happen, claiming that God's will was the only lacking ingredient. Instead of rushing to conclude, "*It must not be his will*," perhaps we should consider that we, like Jesus's disciples, lack the faith to accomplish his will.

Here is the point: faith is not like a light switch that is either on or off. In Mark's version of these events, the father begs Jesus to heal his son if he is able. "Jesus replied, 'Why do you say, "if you can"? Anything is possible for someone who has faith!' At once the boy's father shouted, 'I do have faith! Please help me to have even more'" (Mark 9:23-24 CEV).

Faith can grow. Faith can increase. Faith can become larger. And this is Jesus's will for us—that our faith would grow larger than mustard seeds. God desires for our faith to grow large enough to accomplish impossible things that are his will. Living by faith means exercising our faith muscle to increase its size and strength. Living by faith means that if we follow and trust Jesus, we will do things that are otherwise impossible by our own power, wisdom, and ability. It can be quite daunting, but it is the challenge to which God continually calls us—to live by faith in him.

When was the last time you did something beyond your own ability because of your faith in Jesus? I call this taking the Faith Road.

Like taking the high road, the Faith Road is a choice we make and how we make it. It means looking to God to supply and relying upon the truth of his Word rather than our own feelings, wisdom, or resources. When confronted with a difficult situation, which path do we take? Do we take the path of least resistance? Do we take the path of safety first? Do we take the path of our passions and emotions? Do we take the path of our reason and ability? Or do we take the path of obedience to God's leading, trusting in his power and promises?

The Faith Road follows Jesus into the unknown and trusts him to lead us through.

HEAD POP

A foundational aspect of the training and coaching of our Final 58 Lao national missionary partners in Laos is to help them choose to take the Faith Road. We are blessed when we see those like Ella choose this path. On another occasion, a different team of our Lao national missionary partners demonstrated taking the Faith Road as they went out to share the gospel among the Laoseng people.

Jon, Noy, and Wat arrived at the village of Sukan. This was the same village where our survey team had led the first Laoseng person, Nang, to faith a few months before. Jon, Noy and Wat checked in with the village headman, Surt, when they arrived to pay their respects and make him aware of their activities. Showing respect to the village headman upon arrival is the best way to ensure that he doesn't later oppose anything you do. If the village headman feels disrespected, then you have likely made an unnecessary enemy. In these cases, forgiveness is not easier to obtain than permission. Surt acknowledged their presence and allowed the young men to proceed.

Going through the village on a prayer walk, the team met Bee who had battled chronic illness for years. Many spirit ceremonies and sacrifices had been offered on her behalf, but to no avail. Jon, Noy and Wat shared the gospel message with Bee, and she understood it clearly. She immediately believed and ran to get her husband. He, too, believed in Jesus! Then, suddenly, Bee lost her ability to speak. She tried to talk, but nothing would come out. The team and her family did not know what was happening. Still, Bee ran to fetch her sister and several others to listen to the story that Jon, Noy, and Wat were sharing. In all, about ten new Laoseng people patiently listened to the message from God. Later, Bee recovered her speech.

While this was happening, someone reported to Surt what Jon, Noy, and Wat were doing. When the team returned to his house, they found that he was furious with them. He scolded Jon, Noy, and Wat for sharing the gospel without proper authorization and documentation. He refused to feed them or allow them to stay at his house. He berated them with pointed questions and pushed them toward the edge of the village. Jon, Noy, and Wat suspected that Surt might turn them into the police. Instead, it appeared he was kicking them out of the village. They could easily avoid arrest and possible torture by simply jumping on their motorcycles and leaving. Even Jesus said, "When you are persecuted in one place, flee to another."

However, Jon, Noy, and Wat asked themselves, *What is the faith response? If this is our last time in this village, shouldn't we make the most of it?*

They asked the village headman, "Don't you at least want to know what we were doing?" Surt paused for a moment then demanded, "Yes, explain it to me!"

"We were recounting the story of how God created the world and praying for him to heal people." Jon, Noy, and Wat boldly shared the Creation-to-Christ gospel message with Surt. Slowly, he became less combative. "We can also pray for you, too, if you like," they offered. Surt agreed to allow them to pray for him.

Jon, Noy, and Wat began praying a prayer over the village headman, asking God to bless him and reveal himself to him. As they prayed, Surt felt a pop inside his head, similar to ears popping when changing elevations. This tangible event melted his belligerent attitude toward the team and toward God. Surt felt God's power and immediately wanted to know more.

Jon, Noy, and Wat were surprised to see Surt's countenance when they finished praying. Quickly, he invited them back to his house. Once there, Surt ordered his family to kill a chicken and prepare a meal for the three young men. As they waited to eat, he listened to the team explain more about Jesus and what it means to follow him. "Do you want God?" the team asked Surt. "Yes, I do!" he answered. "What must I do?" Jon, Noy, and Wat prayed with him to receive Christ.

Before the team of national missionaries left Sukan village, Surt invited others to hear the gospel message too. He also invited them to return to the village in the future.

Taking the Faith Road bore fruit for Jon, Noy, and Wat. They could have easily fled when they had the opportunity and would have been justified in doing so. Only faith in the power of God and his gospel caused them to suggest sharing the good news and praying for Surt. They trusted that God's Word would not come back void but accomplish the purpose for which it was sent. When they did, God acted in a way beyond their own ability.

The Faith Road is not a formula. It can't be. As long as God is a part of the equation, we cannot wield his power or control events in spite of his will. But the Faith Road is not spiritual fatalism either, where we resign ourselves to doing nothing but waiting and observing what God may do independent of us. The Faith Road is trusting God while we step out in faith, even when we're unsure where our feet will land.

The Final 58 national missionaries continue to announce the gospel in unreached corners of Laos propelled by faith in a God who is as concerned for these tribes as he was the people of Ninevah in the days of Jonah. Traveling down muddy roads, over mountains, through jungles, and across streams while risking arrest, disease, hunger and persecution is stepping out in faith that God has called and sent them to these peoples. Taking the Faith Road is leading to all the tribes in Laos being reached with the good news of Jesus.

ACTS OF THE LAO APOSTLES

In the last verse of his Gospel, John says, "Jesus did many other things. If they were all written in books, I don't suppose there would be room enough in the whole world for all the books" (John 21:25 CEV). In a similar way, the stories of our Lao national missionaries following the Faith Road to all the unreached tribes in Laos could fill many volumes. There have been both success and failure, suffering and victory. But the work continues, in spite of persecution, stumbling blocks, and pandemics. The gospel is not chained so long as we continue down the Faith Road in the face of any obstacle.

After Luke finished his Gospel, he went on to write another book, the Acts of the Apostles. It has been noted that the book of Acts did not conclude, only stop. When Luke put down his pen, Paul was under house arrest. Yet Luke described Paul's preaching of the gospel message continuing unhindered.

The book of Acts continues until the present time and will continue to be written until Christ's return. Following are short testimonies of how the gospel message continues to be shared along the Faith Road to all the tribes in Laos. Each of these tribes had no witness before our Lao national missionary partners began reaching out to them.

SAMTAO

The Samtao is a tribe of around 3,500 people living in the northern provinces of Luang Nam Tha and Bokeo. In one village, our team of national missionaries led three Samtao people to faith in Christ. Trained to baptize new believers immediately upon understanding and repentance, the national missionaries planned to immerse the new Samtao believers into Christ. Though they received the gospel with joy, they hesitated to take this step. The Samtao believers immediately recognized that baptism was a point-of-no-return decision and they did not want to take it lightly. Our team continued to build up the brand-new believers in Christ, encouraged them to take the step of baptism, and began meeting with them weekly.

KHER

God used two of our female national missionaries, Vaan and Lana, to do a new work among the Kher people. After visiting one Kher village multiple times, several Kher people turned to the Lord. Vaan and Lana taught and discipled these new believers faithfully as they recognized the importance of fanning the small spark into a flame. Their prayer was that the flame would grow and spread to other Kher villages.

In another Kher village, Vaan and Lana took the opportunity to share with a woman who was terribly afraid of the spirits. Her father was a witch doctor, and she peppered Vaan and Lana with questions. After Vaan and Lana shared the complete message of Jesus with the woman, she and both of her parents decided to follow Jesus.

MOUTEUN

Around one thousand Mouteun people live in the northern provinces of Laos. On one occasion, our Lao national missionary partners took a group of visiting Americans to a village they had been attempting to reach but in which they had not seen any fruit. As they walked through the Mouteun village praying, a crazed man began trailing some of the American women on the team. He ate glass and had not bathed in a very long time, among many other strange mannerisms. For the past three years, he had not spoken an intelligible word. As the team dug deeper, the man's parents related how their son had been demon possessed for the last five years. When the family heard of deliverance in Jesus, they expressed interest. A few days later, one of our Lao teams visited this man again without the Americans, and cast the demon out in the authority and power of Jesus's name. The man's first words after three years of silence were "Believe in Christ."

LAOSENG

Our team's work among the Laoseng work got off to a good start in the first village. After they shared the gospel, a man and his family believed. This family grew in faith slowly and steadily as they began worshiping regularly in their home. However, after some time, the old ways held by the rest of the village started to encroach on the family's faith. Village and district officials, in cooperation with police, nearly nabbed one of our teams when they were there to encourage this family. Thankfully, a friend in the village tipped off the team in time. They escaped early the next morning before the police arrived.

Consequently, the work in the first village was paused until things cooled down. From there, the team of national missionaries began work in a second Laoseng village called Boteuk. After only initial efforts to share the good news of Jesus, our national missionary partners led a number of villagers to profess faith in Christ.

Meanwhile, Sone and Mong comprised the team reaching out to the Laoseng village of Sonchua. They established a small group of Christians and returned there regularly to encourage them and build them up in the faith. On one trip, they met the son of one of the elderly believers. This young man had served as a Buddhist monk for six years. Sone and Mong shared the gospel with him. After listening to the entire story, the young monk remarked, "I believe this story is true." He became very excited when his father gave him their copy of the Lao Bible. "I will learn to read the Word of God!" he promised them. Sone and Mong prayed that this monk would sincerely seek the truth and turn to faith in Jesus.

LAOPAN

The Laopan people live in two adjacent villages, called Bangao and Banmai. The people of Bangao first responded enthusiastically to the gospel. However, just as things seemed to be taking off, relatives from Banmai warned them against following Jesus. The opposition discouraged our national missionary team for a time and put the work in limbo. When they returned, some of the Laopan nonbelievers attempted to deny our team entry into the village. One man was particularly hostile toward the work of the gospel in the Laopan villages. However, the young national missionary team did not give up and continued to pray for this man. They repeatedly returned to share God's message with the Laopan people in spite of resistance. This faithful effort kept the fire burning while they prayed for a breakthrough.

YOY

Two of our Lao national missionary partners, Ling and Tone traveled to the Yoy village of Tankam to look for a person of peace and to plant a church. They found one couple with whom they shared the gospel. Ling and Tone rejoiced when the couple decided to follow Christ!

On their next visit to Tankam, Ling and Tone were eager to see if the couple had remained faithful to the Lord. They discovered that the couple had already discarded all their spirit worship paraphernalia and completely left their animistic practices. Ling and Tone were delighted! So, they took the couple to a shallow stream near the village and immersed them in the chilly water. Ling and Tone stayed at the couple's house that night, and Tone encouraged them with his testimony.

From Tankam the team proceeded to the Yoy village of Nadok. There lived a man who had previously listened to the gospel with great interest but felt he was not ready to believe. In spite of his hesitation, the team discovered he had already been sharing about Jesus with his neighbors!

Finally, Ling and Tone continued to two more Yoy villages. They visited some new believers in these villages whom they were discipling. They taught them how to read the Bible, pray, and share a simple gospel presentation.

TRUI

The southern sending base of the Final 58 began engaging the unreached groups there shortly after being established. One of these tribes is the Trui, a sub-tribe of the Bru. Our national missionary team established a beachhead of faith among the Trui. One of the first believers was a Trui woman who wanted to follow the Lord, so they baptized her in a small stream. The water was so shallow that the national missionaries had to lay her down so the water would cover her completely.

Two months later, one of the Trui women gave the growing group of believers a room to use for worship. The Trui church quickly grew to eighteen believers in two villages, which are not far from each other. The believers from both villages began worshiping together every Sunday without fail.

NOOWUR

Pawn and Wat traveled to the Noowur village of Duang. They visited six Noowur people they had previously led to the Lord. Pawn and Wat encouraged their faith and reviewed the story of Jesus with them. They also taught them how to pray. During this discipleship training time, two relatives of the new Noowur believers attended who had not yet heard the message. Pawn and Wat explained the gospel story from creation to Christ's return, and both these relatives decided to put their trust in Jesus too. When they were finished, another man entered the house, so Pawn and Wat shared the gospel with him. He also believed. Finally, this man's father appeared next, and the team shared the gospel yet again. In the end, the father received Christ as well!

JAWHOI

Tavon and Phet were assigned to the Jawhoi people. They returned to

Natonmai village, where twenty-five Jawhoi people had professed faith on their previous visit. Tavon and Phet found themselves swamped with opportunities to share about Christ and many families to visit, teach, and encourage. As they did, they discovered that a few of the new believers there were hoping to forsake only a portion of the spirits they had previously worshiped and continue to placate other spirits with offerings. They were afraid to abandon the lot of them. Consequently, Tavon and Phet spent a great deal of time teaching them about God's power over the evil spirits and that the Jawhoi believers no longer needed to fear them.

BIT

The Bit church continued to grow and prosper in many ways. In the village of Nam Laa, the family of Tongla received Choy and Tawee warmly and slaughtered a chicken to welcome them to dinner. Tongla told them about a neighbor who had injured her knee more than a year before and had never healed. She had gone both to spirit doctors and the hospital, but no one could help her. In the end, she allowed Tongla and other believers to pray for her knee, and she was healed. Choy and Tawee visited this woman and explained the gospel to her again. She didn't believe but was happy to receive the team.

In the weeks before this visit, the provincial governor visited the Bit village to investigate the movement of people to Christ. The presence of a high government official was quite intimidating to those who were still considering following Jesus. As a result, some of them hesitated. But after more prayer by Tongla and additional encouragement from Choy and Tawee, the Bit people relaxed. Tongla was excited that the neighbors who were originally frightened away by the governor's visit were now beginning to show more interest in Jesus.

NGOUAN

Chet and Vawn departed to make another field visit to the Ngouan people, among whom they were sharing the gospel. On their last visit to Kaisou village, they taught three relatives from the Bible. After listening to Chet and Vawn's words, all three made decisions to follow Christ and wanted to be baptized in the morning. The next morning Chet and Vawn baptized the three new believers in a nearby stream.

Chet and Vawn spent the rest of the week in the village with the small

Ngouan church, which quickly grew to nine people. They spent their time teaching the Bible and practicing a simple gospel presentation together. The Ngouan church showed resilience by faithfully worshiping together every Sunday, even when Chet and Vawn were not there to lead them.

PALA

In addition to the Thai Yang and Phousang tribes, Ella and Laa began efforts to reach the Pala people in a remote northern province of Laos. They visited the village of Padong, but almost everyone was away working in their rice fields. Undeterred, Ella and Laa strolled through the village anticipating God to lead them to someone. They met one lame woman whose husband had abandoned her because of her disability. They shared the gospel, explained about God's love, and prayed for her. When they concluded their prayer, the lame woman was able to walk! She decided to put her trust in Jesus after receiving all of these blessings.

JAWHOI AND PILUE

Tavon and Det returned to a Jawhoi village with one family of believers and found the husband bedridden with a serious toothache. After praying for him, the man's wife asked Tavon and Det to leave so that he could rest. By this time, it was dark, and Tavon and Det did not have a place to stay. "Come stay with me!" called a grandfather who recognized them from a previous trip. After dinner, Tavon and Det shared the gospel with this Jawhoi man and his friends. All six of them believed in Jesus before going to bed that night!

The following day, Tavon and Det traveled to a Pilue village. They shared the message of Christ with an old man who listened but rejected the message. Just then, a woman limped up to them. "Can you pray for my injured knee?" she asked. After prayer, she felt much better, so other villagers lined up to receive prayer as well. Many were healed. In the end, five Pilue people decided to follow Jesus, including an educated former government official.

JIPEA

Two of our Lao national missionary partners, Van and Mong, visited Boonma village belonging to the Jipea tribe. They shared the gospel boldly, and many people were interested, but not ready to forsake their old practices of worshiping the spirits. However, one older man listened attentively and later asked Van and Mong to explain the gospel a second time. In the end, he and his son decided to follow Jesus.

Two weeks later, Van and Mong returned to Boonma village, where the two Jipea men had believed on their last trip. Another man was visiting the new believers, so Mong shared the gospel with him. This man became the third Jipea Christian in the village.

Later, Van and Mong found another man with whom they shared the gospel. This man warned them, "Two guys were here a couple weeks ago talking about Jesus, and the headman called the police on them. But the police arrived just after they left." Van and Mong realized they were the two men to whom he was referring, though the man who warned them did not know. On their previous trip, they had seen police driving into the village as they departed. Van and Mong gave thanks to God for his protection.

In another Jipea village, a man and his son listened raptly to the gospel while Van and Mong shared, and both believed. "Don't go anywhere!" they implored Van and Mong. "We'll make a big lunch and invite more friends so you can share this message with them too!"

There are still many more tribes in Laos who have yet to hear the story of how God created the world and sent his son to offer his life as payment for our sins so that we can be reconciled to our father in heaven and become a part of his holy and loving family. Each morning they rise to work in their fields living with sickness and fear and knowing no other way than to placate the tormenting spirits in hope of some relief. When our national missionaries consider the honor of being the one with the "beautiful feet" to tell them about Jesus, such that some from each of these tribes will be present in front of the Lamb on the last day, they know all the pain, discomfort, trials, and persecution are very much worth it!

How may God be calling you to step out in faith on their behalf?

ALL THE TRIBES

THE HASTENING

I rolled my eyes. A friend of mine forwarded a link of utmost importance. According to an updated reading of the Mayan calendar, the world was set to end the following Sunday. I must read and share!

Sunday came and went. Nothing unusual happened.

Years earlier, Mali and I visited a Lao Christian friend of ours in Bangkok. He was involved with a church there that just received a visit from an American prophet. She was claiming that Christ's return would happen by the end of the year. It was 2005. Our friend was excited and said that many people are coming to church to hear this prophet.

An eye roll wasn't enough. I felt disturbed by the effect "calling wolf" has upon believers. The short-term gain of attendance (and offerings) is demolished by their disillusionment later on. In the end, it is a great way to get people to turn *away* from Christ—promise things you can't deliver, so that when you finally disappoint them, they throw out God along with you. Next time, they don't even want to listen.

I asked my Lao friend, "Do you know that Jesus said that no one knows the day or the hour of his return? Not even the angels, or Jesus himself? Only God the Father knows." My friend was aware of the scripture in Matthew 24:36. "If the Father doesn't even tell Jesus when the date is, why would he tell this woman?" I challenged. My friend admitted it was a good point. I explained that Jesus foretold of many false prophets in the last days in that same passage of scripture. Many trials and persecution will happen before he comes, and many will give up on their faith, but our job is to stand firm until the end. This is what Jesus told us in Matthew 24:13. No matter what happens, we must persist in our faith until the very end.

"Calling wolf" has another effect upon those of us who are prone to roll our eyes at every doomsday prediction. It lulls us into discounting the second coming of Christ as anything imminent. *Surely, we will all die natural deaths long before Christ comes to judge the inhabitants of this earth.* In our minds, we have pushed it so far out into the future that we subconsciously (and theologically) forget that an end is coming at all.

However, it *is* coming. Jesus told us so. It is also relevant. It is relevant in terms of where we place our hope. Our hope is not that our society will evolve to the point that one day we will have achieved our own utopia. On the contrary, our hope is in the new kingdom that Christ will establish. If our hope is in the "more perfect union" we are building, we will invest our energies and efforts into the current system. However, if our hope is in Christ and the kingdom to come, we will invest our efforts into preparing people to receive his kingdom. Namely, we will join with Jesus to complete his mission. This is the same mission Jesus entrusted to the apostle Paul in the book of Acts:

> I am sending you to them to open their eyes and turn them from darkness to light, and from the power of Satan to God, so that they may receive forgiveness of sins and a place among those who are sanctified by faith in me. (Acts 26:17b-18 NIV)

When Jesus commissioned his followers in Matthew 28, he told them to "make disciples of all nations." It has been noted that the Greek word used for nations in this passage is *ethne*. *Ethne* is the root word for 'ethnic' and does not refer to geopolitical nations (countries) as we know them today but is more closely associated with what we would call ethnic groups or tribes. Jesus was commanding his followers to make disciples of all the tribes in the world.

In Luke's version of the Great Commission, in the first chapter of Acts, Jesus announced to his followers, "You will be my witnesses in Jerusalem, and in all Judea and Samaria, and to the ends of the earth" (Acts 1:8b NIV). There is an obvious progression to his words, starting from their location, spreading outward, and reaching the ends of the earth.

The task Jesus gave to his church was enormous but not infinite. He did not simply give them an ongoing activity—he gave them a task that could be completed and that one day would be. In fact, Jesus refers to the completion of this same task—being his witnesses to the ends of the earth and to all nations—in the same chapter of Matthew where he said no one knows the day and hour of his return:

And this gospel of the kingdom will be preached in the whole world as a testimony to all nations [*ethne*], and then the end will come. Matthew 24:14 (NIV)

Jesus doesn't tell us, or even know, the day or the hour the end will come, but he tells us the order in which it will happen. First—his mission is completed; then—he comes.

Though we don't know the date, Peter reveals that we can "hasten" the return of Christ. In 2 Peter 3:11b-12a (NIV) he says, "You ought to live holy and godly lives as you look forward to the day of God and speed its coming." How can we speed his coming?

Earlier in the same chapter, Peter says, "The Lord is not slow in keeping his promise as some understand slowness. Instead he his patient with you, not wanting anyone to perish, but everyone to come to repentance" (2 Peter 3:9 NIV).

We already discussed the slowness complaint that Peter was addressing here. Early Christians were wondering why Jesus had not yet returned. The answer is that he is patient and doesn't want anyone to perish. Once he returns, it will be too late. So, he is not rushing to return because he wants more people to have the opportunity to repent and be saved!

But with whom is he being patient? It's easy to read this verse that God is being patient with all the people who have yet to repent. *What is taking them so long?!* Actually, Peter says that God is being patient with *you*. God is being patient with the readers of Peter's letter.

To whom was Peter writing his letter? Both 1 and 2 Peter are known as general epistles because they are epistles (letters) written to Christians in general and not just Christians in one locality or church. So, if Peter is writing to Christians, we can assume they have already repented, been forgiven, and are saved from perishing in hell. So, why is God being patient with the Christians if he wants no one to perish but all to come to repentance?

The answer is clear. Christ's followers are the ones God gave the awesome privilege and responsibility to share his Good News with all the tribes on earth. He blessed us so that we could be a blessing. They will only hear this message when we tell them. So, God is not being patient with the unrepentant, waiting for them to repent, so much as he is being patient with the church, waiting for us to offer this message of forgiveness of sins in Jesus to all people who are still in darkness.

PRAY

"Wait, wait!" Felipe pleaded. We had just finished praying and were about to leave for a village in the backwoods of David, Panama. It was 1995, and we were planting a church in an unreached town along with our Panamanian brothers and sisters. Each week we took turns preaching, and tonight Felipe was up to bat. He stopped us in our tracks. "I am teaching tonight. We need to pray that God will speak through me!" Felipe had us gather back around in a circle, bow our heads, and pray for him.

I chuckled internally when I saw Felipe insist that we pray a second time. *We already prayed*, I thought, *is it really necessary to pray again? He thinks a prayer is going to make a difference.*

The second thought startled me. *Wait—don't I believe that prayer makes a difference?*

I would have always claimed that prayer is important and effectual. However, my initial reaction to Felipe betrayed a lack of faith in my own heart. If I had been speaking that night and the group had forgotten to pray for me, I would not have called everyone back a second time. I would have proceeded and just said a prayer in my own heart. But Felipe felt it was important enough to interrupt the social momentum and call everyone back to pray. He knew that prayer makes a difference and did not want to go into spiritual battle without it. I, on the other hand, would have been content to fight out of my own flesh hoping that God would intervene if needed.

Prayer is an act of faith. We pray; God moves. Why does he not always move the instant we pray? People have debated this mystery for ages. I do not claim to know all the answers. It is no secret, however, that he wants us to pray. Jesus told the parable of the persistent widow to show his disciples how "they should always pray and not give up" (Luke 18:1 NIV).

What does he want us to pray for?

It is possible that you pray for your "daily bread" and your needs, both physical and spiritual. You likely pray for your relationships and loved ones, as well as for help to live a godly life. You pray that you will not be led into temptation.

Do you also pray for God's name to be honored as holy on earth? ("Hallowed be your name.")

Do you pray for God's kingdom to be established among the unreached? ("Your kingdom come.")

Do you pray that all people will completely obey God and his commands? ("Your will be done on earth as it is in heaven.")

In what we now call the Lord's Prayer (Matthew 6:9-13 NIV) the first three requests he taught us to pray are things that *he* wants for himself—for his name to be honored as holy (hallowed), for his kingdom to be established, and for his will to be obeyed. Could it be that he wants us to *want* these things more than we want our daily bread?

I believe that God teaches us to persist in prayer and withholds his actions at least some of the time while we beseech him because he wants us to care about the things he cares about. He wants us to have a heart for the things he has a heart for.

You don't just pray for the things about which you care; you care about the things for which you pray.

In addition to the Lord's Prayer, what else does Jesus tell us to pray for?

If you remember, Jesus also commanded us to pray for our enemies and for those who persecute us. In light of the opposition our Lao national missionary partners receive from the police, government authorities, shamans, and non-believers, it is important that we follow Jesus's command to pray for all of these people. Pray that God will melt their hearts of stone. Pray that God will bring light to their dark minds.

Finally, there is one more thing about which Jesus told us to pray:

Jesus went to every town and village. He taught in their meeting places and preached the good news about God's kingdom. Jesus also healed every kind of disease and sickness. When he saw the crowds, he felt sorry for them. They were confused and helpless, like sheep without a shepherd. He said to his disciples, "A large crop is in the fields, but there are only a few workers. Ask the Lord in charge of the harvest to send out workers to bring it in." (Matthew 9:35-38 CEV)

Jesus often compared the work of sharing the good news of his kingdom to a farmer planting a crop. The sharing is the sowing, and the harvest is the leading of people to enter Christ's kingdom by believing and repenting. But Jesus said there were not enough people to do this job. Therefore, we must "ask the Lord in charge of the harvest" to send more (Matthew 9:38 CEV). Jesus is telling us to pray for the work of his mission—the work to seek and save the lost.

Never has a huge movement of God happened without extraordinary prayer. Many have documented that throughout the history of missions every major missionary effort and breakthrough was born out of prayer. When Christians bow to pray like Jesus told us, the kingdom advances. All Christians around the globe can play a part in his mission in this way. All the tribes in Laos that have now heard the gospel never would have been reached if it weren't for faithful followers of Jesus lifting them up in prayer. And all the tribes in Laos who have yet to hear will not turn to Jesus unless we plead with him on their behalf.

James Fraser, a pioneer missionary to the Lisu people of the upper Mekong region in southern China, wrote about the importance of prayer a century ago:

> I feel my weakness very much, yet the Lord seems to delight in making His power perfect in weakness. May I ask you then to remember me especially in prayer, asking God to use me to the salvation of many precious souls? I am feeling more and more that it is, after all, just the prayers of God's people that call down blessing upon the work, whether they are directly engaged in it or not. Paul may plant and Apollos water, but it is God who gives the increase; and this increase can be brought down from heaven by believing prayer.... We do our part, and then can only look to Him, with others, for His blessing. If this is so, then Christians at home can do as much for foreign missions as those actually on the field. I believe it will only be known on the Last Day how much has been accomplished in missionary work by the prayers of earnest believers at home.... Solid, lasting missionary work is done on our knees. What I covet more than anything else is earnest, believing prayer, and I write to ask you to continue to put up much prayer for me and the work here.[1]

---

1. Geraldine Taylor, Behind the Ranges: The Life-Changing Story of J.O. Fraser (Singapore: OMF International (IHQ) Ltd., 1998), 52.

In the same way, I covet your earnest prayers for all the tribes in Laos and beyond. Will you ask the Lord of the harvest on their behalf?

SEND

Jim Elliot was a missionary to Ecuador in South America when he was killed by a band of Waorani warriors (known as the Auca at the time) in 1958. *Through Gates of Splendor* and *Shadow of the Almighty*, two accounts of Jim's story as told by his widow, Elisabeth Elliot, were formative narratives for me as I considered joining the ranks of foreign missionaries sent out from the American church. Jim's passion for Christ and for the unreached inspired me. He famously wrote in his journal, "He is no fool who gives what he cannot keep to gain what he cannot lose."[2] Jim was determined not to become one of the 90 percent of people who committed to missionary service at Christian conferences, only never to make it to the mission field.

Like many other missionary recruits, as the time approached for Jim to leave, some well-meaning people tried to dissuade him. One of those was his mother. She loved her son and didn't want to see him move so far away or face the perils of life in the jungle. She knew she could never alter his passion for Christ, so instead of trying to discourage the idea directly, she asked Jim to consider the need for Christian ministry in the US.

I have heard many of my missionary colleagues tell me they faced similar arguments. People who loved them didn't want to see them go. They provided many good reasons why it was unnecessary and how they could serve the Lord just as passionately much closer to home. "America has a lot of needs too!"

I have joked that I did not face the same level of opposition when it was time for me to leave. Instead, people approached me and said, "Eliot, we think God is calling you to become a missionary. Yeah, we think he wants you to move far, far away!"

The truth is many more people need to go than do. Yes, there are needs everywhere, but the needs of the lost in the most unreached regions of earth far exceed the ability of the church in those places to address them. Jim Elliot said, "If you see ten men carrying a log, nine of them on one end, on which end will you help out?"[3] Yet, for everyone who goes, there must be a community of people to send him or her too.

2. Elisabeth Elliot, Shadow of the Almighty (New York: HarperCollins, 1989), 108.
3. Elisabeth Elliot, letter to the author, May 30, 1996.

In talking about unreached peoples in Romans 10:14-15 (NIV), Paul says:

How, then, can they call on the one they have not believed in? And how can they believe in the one of whom they have not heard? And how can they hear without someone preaching to them? And how can anyone preach unless they are sent? As it is written: "How beautiful are the feet of those who bring good news!"

Paul's argument still causes my heart to thump inside my chest. If people put their trust in Jesus, they will be saved. But there is no way for them to put their trust in him if they have never heard about him. And there is no way for them to hear about him if no one goes to tell them. And there is no way for people to go to them unless someone *sends* them!

Beyond the tithes and offerings you give to your local congregation, what are you doing to send missionaries to unreached peoples? If you cannot go yourself, can you recruit others for the task? Can you disciple those who have been recruited to go? Can you support them financially to do God's work?

The work of national missionaries in the Final 58 project and other projects in Southeast Asia is some of the most cutting-edge mission work happening on the globe. On one hand, we are not just sending out Western missionaries who require an enormous investment of resources and time to learn the language, and on the other hand, we are not sending out nationals void of any training or accountability. However, we are mobilizing national missionaries who have been vetted, trained, and mobilized as a part of an intentional system of strategy and coaching so that the gospel will be effectively planted among the unreached.

Many on the outside do their part to help send out these fruitful workers. Yet more senders are needed too. Does God have a role for you to play in sending out those with beautiful feet?

GO

The year was 1993. I was about to graduate from college. As I walked across campus, I ran in to Craig—an old friend from high school. We caught up a bit and then the topic turned to post-graduation. "What are you going to do?" he asked me. "My plan is to become a missionary and share the love of

Christ with those who have never heard," I answered. I could tell the idea was strange to my friend, even though he was a Christian. *It's not every day you meet an oddball who wants to do something like that!*

"You know," my friend responded with incredulity," I saw a show about a nomadic tribe in Africa. When they were interviewed, the topic of religion came up, and they had never heard of Jesus! It's amazing that nearly two thousand years since he was born there is still a tribe out there that has never heard the gospel!"

"Oh, Craig," I said, astounded, "It's not just one tribe. It's more than half the world!"

Craig had no idea.

Over the years, I have found that many Christians are like Craig—they just assume that everyone on earth has already heard about Jesus. Consequently, there is little connection in people's minds between the progress of missionary efforts and the conclusion of world history. If the world has already been saturated with the gospel, there is nothing other than politics to keep our eyes on. Indeed, many are much more interested and aware of what is going on in the world politically than they are regarding kingdom work.

Many, like my friend Craig, assume there are only a few remnant villages of tribes in the Amazon that don't yet know the gospel. While it is true that many people around the world have heard of a religion called Christianity, hundreds of millions of them still haven't heard enough about Jesus to make a decision to become his disciples. And many have still not even heard his name. Both are considered unreached.

A friend from Illinois visited me when I lived in the northern province of Bokeo, Laos. Near the city was a single village of Lanten people. Most of the Lanten lived hours away in Luang Nam Tha province, but for one reason or another, these Lanten people had migrated to Bokeo. While many tribal groups adopted the dress and style of the wider Lao culture, the Lanten maintained their traditional clothing and unique house construction. Consequently, it was an interesting village to which to take visitors.

My Lao language ability was just getting to the point that I could communicate about complex topics, though the accent and broken Lao of the rural minorities made it a challenge. The Lanten village headman took us around the village, and I translated for my guest. At one point, I had the opportunity to share about Christ with the headman, but he was unaware of the Lao term for Jesus—Pha Yesu. I repeated it slowly, so that he could understand. "I'm sorry," the headman replied. "He doesn't live here in our village." He had no idea who I was talking about. He had never even heard the name of Jesus. And his village was not very remote.

"Here it is!" I announced to my friend, gesturing to the village. "Here is an example of a completely unreached tribe that has never heard the good news of Jesus." The village was just a ten-minute drive from town.

Thankfully, because of the work of our national missionary partners in Laos, these tribes are being reached. But there are still many more—in Laos, in Southeast Asia, and on most continents of the world. (I'm pretty sure Antarctica is reached.) Like my friend Craig, it is easy not to see them. It is easy not to realize they are there and to assume they have already heard the message. They are easy to ignore. But there are still more than seven thousand unreached tribes, or *ethne*, in our world today.

God sees them. His eyes are on them. He has not forgotten them. He has not gotten sidetracked from the same mission he gave his apostles nearly two thousand years ago.

How is God calling you to join him in his mission to open their eyes, to turn them from darkness to light, and from the power of Satan to God, so that they may receive forgiveness of sins and a place among those who are sanctified by faith in Jesus?

Do you know what else God sees? He sees you. Yes, you.

"Nah—I could never be a missionary!" you may think. "I'm too old. I have too many responsibilities. I'm not trained. I'm too quick-tempered. I'm a sinner. I'm unsure. I'm not good at speaking. I'm no one special." This very well may be.

If so, then you are like Abraham, Paul, all of Jesus's disciples, James and John, Peter, Thomas, Moses and David.

"No, they were extraordinary people—Bible heroes. I'm just an ordinary person. It's just not possible."

You may be ordinary. However, all these people were used by God not because they were extraordinary but because they had faith in a God who was. He is the same God who sees you, sees your heart, and knows everything about you. He is just as extraordinary now as he was back then. And with faith in him, nothing is impossible.

All the tribes await. Will you step out onto the Faith Road?

SAILING AND SERVING

"**U**nless the LORD builds the house, the builders labor in vain. Unless the LORD watches over the city, the guards stand watch in vain" Psalm 127:1 (NIV).

Sail boating is mostly a recreational activity anymore. In the past, before steam and internal combustion engines, sailing was the only way to cross the ocean. Huge vessels carried goods, travelers, pilgrims, immigrants, supplies, artillery, and treasure. And they traversed the globe all on the power of the wind.

Now we don't depend upon the wind—at least not for trade, travel, and commerce. Our engines are more reliable. On the stillest of days, we can power our way ahead. We don't have to wait until the wind blows. Additionally, powered by fossil fuels, we can set our course straight to our destination without tacking no more than twenty-two degrees from the wind's direction. In fact, we can even push our way directly into the wind. Our innovations have made sailing obsolete—no waiting and no limit to the direction of our heading.

We can go wherever we want, when we want. So, why wait on the wind? Again, sailing is now relegated to those who just want to play around and have fun.

Jesus said to Nicodemus, "The wind blows wherever it pleases. You hear its sound, but you cannot tell where it comes from or where it is going. So it is with everyone born of the Spirit" (John 3:8 NIV).

The Spirit of God is often compared to the wind. As such, he is uncontrollable and unpredictable. For this reason, he makes many of us uncomfortable. *When will God move? Which way will he lead us? What if he is silent and still? What if he blows in a direction we don't want to go?*

For these reasons, it can be very difficult to wait upon the Lord—especially in "professional" ministry. People expect results if you're living on "God's money." It becomes much easier to make ministry plans like business plans—to satisfy investors and to guarantee results!

I've become leery of ministry plans and approaches that implicitly assert, "We are going to be successful with or without God's help! We don't need to rely upon him because we have a formula and recipe for success!"

When we do this, we are relying upon ourselves and our own innovations, rather than God. We betray our lack of faith that God will move at some point even when he is silent now. We admit that we *don't* rely upon God because we feel we *can't* rely upon him—he is not dependable. When will he come through for us? It's as if we're saying, "God, here's our plan we will execute for you. If you want to show up and bless it, that would be great! But even if you don't, we know we can succeed!"

It reminds me of rhetoric I hear sometimes insisting that a specific ministry technique is the engine of a movement of God. It reasons that the process of reproduction is built into the DNA of the methodology, and as long as people work the process, it will produce generational growth.

I suppose if you have a powerful engine that will take you where you need to go, you no longer need to put your sail up and wait for any wind to blow.

Can we rely upon God for real ministry results, or is doing so only for those with the luxury to play around in God's kingdom?

I love to plan and develop strategies. I think these things are valuable and have their place. But I am challenged by his Spirit to put up my sails and wait upon the Lord, to hear from him, and to avoid the temptation to engage in activities designed primarily to impress and satisfy the investors or to get things done according to a predetermined course. Yes, I believe the Word of God gives us the parameters of how God works, but even within the bounds of scripture, there is plenty of room for the wind to blow.

This book is not a prescription about how to have missionary or ministry success. Feel free to borrow ideas and strategies and apply them as you see fit, but please know that I am not advocating for a narrowly defined strategy, approach, or methodology. I am not selling a program. Neither am I claiming to have the "secret sauce" to missionary success, other than what the Lord has already asked us to do: have faith, go, make disciples, baptize, obey, love, be persistent, and pray.

I admit I am passionate about the principles of reproducibility, non-dependency, and avoiding the ruts of traditional approaches. I believe these incredibly important issues are too often overlooked in missions. Yet I am not advocating for any specific cookie-cutter program that attempts to address these issues. I believe it is important to look at each context, rely upon our knowledge of scripture, and put up our sails to see where God leads.

Instead of a prescription, this book is a description of what God has shown me. It is an account of how he has led and what he has done through his faithful partners, who will never become famous on earth. It is a testimony, not a formula, a narrative, not a recipe. As such, it is my hope that this testimony will inspire you to seek him more passionately, love him more deeply, and serve him more intentionally. And it is my prayer that you will give your life to the completion of *his* mission.

GROUP STUDY GUIDE
THE FAITH ROAD

Chapter 1: THE RED THUMB SOCIETY

1. What is the distinction that Eliot makes between dogs and tigers?

2. Eliot could not sleep because he was anxious about the imminent police interrogation. Have you ever worried about an impending confrontation? How did it affect you?

3. Pastor Khan's words moved Eliot to tears. What was it that touched him so deeply? How was it different from the encouragement he received on Facebook? How might you apply this when responding to those in your life who face difficult situations?

4. Read Revelation 6:9-11. What are the implications of this verse to the mission of the church and the conclusion of world history? How might this impact you?

5. Eliot says, "Enduring opposition has been the modus operandi for the church throughout the ages. A short history of Christian preference and prominence in the US is more of an anomaly than a historical status quo. But it has lulled some Christians into expecting an easy road. The Bible promises that if we wish to live a godly life we will be persecuted (2 Timothy 3:12). There is no way around it. The only way to live a comfortable Christian life, safe from persecution, is never to be a threat to Satan." In what ways can you increase your threat to Satan?

6. What are other ways God spoke to you through this chapter? What do you
   feel him leading you to do?

Chapter 2: JESUS SAW ME

1. Have you ever witnessed a miracle? Do you think it would help your faith if
   you did? Why or why not? Why do you think God showed Eliot the meteor
   as he requested?

2. Early in his life, Eliot struggled to see his own worth to others and to God.
   In what ways is this a common struggle? Do you feel you measure up to the
   world's standard of wealth, beauty, charisma and talent?

3. Read Psalm 8:1-9. What do these verses say about how God values people
   in comparison to the rest of his creation?

4. Have you ever had a time in your life when you felt that Jesus saw you?
   Describe that experience. If not, is it something you desire?

5. On his first trip to Laos, Eliot envisioned two images of Jesus while riding
   his bicycle. In what ways are you inspired by envisioning how Jesus would
   interact with others you encounter in your life?

6. What are other ways God spoke to you through this chapter? What do you
   feel him leading you to do?

Chapter 3: SECOND CONVERSION

1. Eliot described a significant paradigm shift when Kaosing shared his perspective with him regarding the politeness of Lao people. Have you ever listened to another perspective and, after doing so, come to a completely different point of view?

2. What are your feelings about the social hierarchy Eliot described in Lao society? How strongly do you feel that equal value requires equal social status?

3. Do you feel it is difficult to respect another culture when that culture has a different value system? How might considering cultural differences help you to evaluate your own culture more objectively?

4. Eliot described becoming the object of Pastor Nokeo's projection and the prevalence of projection, both positive and negative, in misinterpreting cross-cultural situations. What insights did you gain from this discussion? What do you think it takes to get an accurate interpretation of another culture?

5. Read Matthew 16:24-26. What is required to follow Jesus? How did Eliot's second conversion represent a losing of life for Jesus? How may Jesus be calling you to lose your life for him?

6. What are other ways God spoke to you through this chapter? What do you feel him leading you to do?

Chapter 4: THE MIEN

1. What were some of the answers to prayer that God provided Eliot and others in this chapter? How have you seen God move after prayer? Have you ever felt that prayer does not work? Why or why not?

2. Pastor Tsoi's father disowned him when he became a Christian. Have you ever faced opposition from loved ones because of your faith in Jesus?

3. What were the spiritual problems that Tanva and Nai Fong had which made them open to faith in Jesus? Who in your life has situations that may make them more open to becoming Christians?

4. After leaving Ketpu village, Eliot was discouraged because he could not see how unreached people there would ever accept the Lord. Have you ever felt completely discouraged or that God could not work in a particularly challenging situation? Have you ever seen him work in spite of this? What does it take to trust God and go beyond your limits?

5. Read 2 Chronicles 20:15. What reason does this verse give for overcoming fear and discouragement? What is our job, then?

6. What are other ways God spoke to you through this chapter? What do you feel him leading you to do?

Chapter 5: EARLY PERILS

1. Eliot was detained and interrogated for passing out the gospel coins. In what ways did God protect him during this experience?

2. When Kanpet was in the refugee camp, he assumed he would join the majority who went on to live in the US. However, the missionary challenged him to return to Laos with the good news. How might God challenge you to make a major life decision for the sake of others rather than for your own benefit?

3. Eliot did not want to endure police interrogation in Sainyabuli with his children in tow. Do you think this was a good decision? Why or why not? What may have been gained by "facing the music"? What may have been lost? In what ways is it possible to hide behind our loved ones to escape hardship and persecution?

4. Read Isaiah 43:1-3. Does God promise to prevent suffering and trials if we follow him? What is his promise?

5. Read Isaiah 49:6. In what ways may God be saying that your goals and vision, though they are good, are too small? How may he be calling you to something greater?

6. What are other ways God spoke to you through this chapter? What do you feel him leading you to do?

Chapter 6: MULTIPLY

1. What exactly is the gap that Eliot describes in the first part of chapter 6? What stands out to you about this insight?

2. What do you think is the main point about the mango tree example? What lesson can we take from this and apply to our lives in light of God's purpose on earth?

3. Did the example of Mr. Big and Mr. Little surprise you? Eliot admits that both examples are unrealistic; however, what are the important lessons we can take away from this parable?

4. What are the differences between an institutional view of the church and a missional view?

5. Read Matthew 13:1-9, 18-23. Of the four described, which types of soil best help God accomplish his mission? What weeds in your life may you need to remove to become fruitful?

6. What are other ways God spoke to you through this chapter? What do you feel him leading you to do?

Chapter 7: BIRTH OF THE FINAL 58

1. Why does the gospel not readily flow to hidden groups of people? What are the barriers?

2. When presented with the challenge to reach all the tribes in Laos, Eliot said he decided to approach the effort from the basis of abundance rather than poverty. In what ways do we limit God and ourselves when making plans based upon the level of resources we have at our disposal? How might we plan differently if we took into account all the resources God has at his disposal?

3. Eliot did not want to recruit the wrong people to become national missionaries. How did he overcome this challenge? How might this apply to someone looking to partner with you?

4. What is dependency? How does dependency become a common pitfall when Western missionaries partner with Christians in impoverished locations? How do we best avoid this pitfall?

5. Read 1 Thessalonians 2:1-12 and 2 Thessalonians 3:6-10. What is Paul's example and command to the Thessalonian believers? How can we apply this in our lives?

6. What are other ways God spoke to you through this chapter? What do you feel him leading you to do?

Chapter 8: FAITH JOURNEY

1. Why did the Final 58 Faith Journey participants not bring enough food and money with them? Why were they encouraged *not* to ask for food and lodging?

2. Eliot says, "Faith is like a muscle. The only way to grow it is to use it." Do you agree with this? In what ways can you grow in your faith by using it?

3. From your own knowledge of the stories of Jesus in Matthew, Mark, Luke, and John, in what ways did Jesus prepare his disciples for ministry? How did Jesus help them grow in their faith?

4. Read Luke 10:1-9. How did this "mission trip" stretch the faith of Jesus's disciples?

5. Do you think your church or Christian fellowship group could do a similar kind of Faith Journey in your context? What might it look like?

6. What are other ways God spoke to you through this chapter? What do you feel him leading you to do?

Chapter 9: FIRSTFRUITS

1. What was Samuel Hatt's role in the mission of the Final 58? How significant were his actions? Do you think it made a difference?

2. As Teo and Boonmi surveyed villages and tribes in Laos, they found an opportunity to share the gospel. They made the most of this opportunity, and Nang came to faith as a result. As you go about the work you do, what opportunities do you have to share about Jesus with others? Do you ever miss these opportunities because you are focused upon your job or the task at hand?

3. Eliot said, "We felt strongly that the groups we did confirm should not wait to hear about Jesus while we spent our time and resources looking for unconfirmed groups." Do you sense the urgency to begin doing what God has called you to do? Have you possibly delayed your participation in order to better prepare yourself? What is the appropriate level and length of preparation?

4. Compare the actions of Tawee and Lat on their first night in the Bit village when they saw there was a drunken festival. How might we miss opportunities because it seems that any effort would be a waste of time?

5. Read Acts 19:13-20. Do you think it was easy for the new believers to confess what they had done and to burn their items of sorcery? For the unreached animist villagers being reached in Laos, how significant was it for them to break with their spirit worship practices and burn their items? Is there anything in your life, secret or costly, that you need to destroy or surrender to God?

6. What are other ways God spoke to you through this chapter? What do you feel him leading you to do?

Chapter 10: OPPOSITION

1. What stood out to you most about Daa and Nok's story? What were the main ways they handled their arrest well?

2. Under threat of execution and fear of rape, Daa and Nok spent the night in the ramshackle latrine cell. As they tried to sleep in the horrid conditions, they meditated on scripture. Why was this the right thing to do? How can reminding yourself of God's truth help you to endure difficult situations?

3. Read John 4:1-42. How were the Samaritans a hidden people to the disciples? Why did Jesus not eat when the disciples invited him to join them? What did Jesus see that they missed?

4. What is your view of suffering? What does the Bible teach us about suffering? How does being on the same page with Jesus help us to endure opposition?

5. In the face of opposition, some of the Phousang believers recanted their faith. The Makong Pua believers, however, stood firm. What was the result of these two paths? Is it better to recant one's faith and later be reinstated, like Peter, or never to recant at all? Why?

6. What are other ways God spoke to you through this chapter? What do you feel him leading you to do?

Chapter 11: THE FAITH ROAD

1. Ella faced two crises of faith—one with the police and one with the Christian pastor who begged her to abandon her role as a national missionary. Which of these afforded her the opportunity to take the Faith Road? In your opinion, which of these were a bigger threat to what God wanted to accomplish?

2. Eliot says that faith is not like a light switch, turned either off or on, but that it can grow. Do you agree with this view of faith? How is it supported or not supported by scripture? How can you grow your faith?

3. When you pray and God does not grant what you have requested, how can you determine if it was not his will or if you lack faith?

4. What does it mean to take the Faith Road? How does it differ from taking the path of least resistance, the path of emotions, the path of reason or ability? What is the faith response to situations you face in your life?

5. Read Acts 20:17-38. Paul was on his way to Jerusalem. What would happen to Paul there? In what ways did Paul take the Faith Road in his ministry (as described in this scripture) and on his way to Jerusalem?

6. What are other ways God spoke to you through this chapter? What do you feel him leading you to do?

Chapter 12: ALL THE TRIBES

1. How much do you think about the second coming of Jesus? Do you tend to think it is very near or in the distant future?

2. Read 2 Peter 3:1-13. How is the mission God gave us connected to the conclusion of world history? How relevant is this to our life and faith now?

3. Read Matthew 9:35-38. What does this tell you about God's heart? Eliot says, "You don't just pray for the things about which you care; you care about the things for which you pray." Could Jesus be asking us to pray for more workers because he wants us to care about the harvest as much as he does?

4. Read Romans 10:11-15. How important is it for the church to send out missionaries? How can you be involved in sending?

5. Read Luke 5:1-11. Peter was not one of the crowd following and listening to Jesus, but just happened to be there cleaning his nets. He objected to Jesus's request to go fishing but complied. After he saw the miraculous catch of fish, Peter begged Jesus to go away. Why did Jesus not listen to him? How might you be pushing Jesus away when he is calling you to something greater?

6. What are other ways God spoke to you through this chapter? What do you feel him leading you to do?

Postscript: SAILING AND SERVING

1. What is the essential difference between sailboats and steamboats according to Eliot's description? How does this relate to the way we live our lives and serve the Lord?

2. According to this metaphor, if the Holy Spirit is the wind, how can we put up our sails to catch the direction and force with which God is leading us?

3. What is the difference between description and prescription? Why might some people be tempted to boil ministry down to a recipe or formula? What do we miss when we do this?

4. "We are going to be successful with or without God's help!" Do you ever feel tempted to plan in such a way? Does following God's leading mean we discard all strategic thinking and planning?

5. Read Psalm 127:1. What is this scripture calling us to do? How can we apply it in practice?

6. What are other ways God spoke to you through this postscript? What do you feel him leading you to do?

NOTE FROM THE PUBLISHER

Proceeds from the sale of this book go toward the ministry of Mekong Multiply, whose mission is to support the work of near-neighbor and national missionaries multiplying disciples and churches among unreached people groups in Southeast Asia and beyond.

If you have interest in supporting the ministry of Mekong Multiply, adopting an unreached people group, or sponsoring a national missionary to multiply disciples and churches, please contact us at missions@mekongmultiply.com or visit our website at www.mekongmultiply.com.